10-16

Unlikely
Friendships®
DOGS

Unlikely Friendships® DOGS

37 STORIES *of* CANINE COMPASSION *and* COURAGE

by

JENNIFER S. HOLLAND

WORKMAN PUBLISHING · NEW YORK

Library of Congress Cataloging-in-Publication Data is available.

ISBN 978-0-7611-8728-8

Layout by Ariana Abud
Design by Raquel Jaramillo

Photo Credits:
Cover: Luiz Higa Junior/Caters News Agency Ltd.
Back Cover: Fran Stothard / SWNS.com (Top) Les Wilson/Rex/Shutterstock (Bottom)
Courtesy of AMVQ—Serge Vaillancourt: p. 23; **Associated Press**—Ted S. Warren: p. 100; **Jim Ballou:** pp. 138, 140, 141, 143, 144, 145; **Courtesy of Christy Bergen:** p. 227; **Bond/360:** pp. 170, 173; **Courtesy of Jackie Borum:** pp. 210, 213, 214 (all), 215; **Dorothée Brand:** pp. 222, 225; **Tanja Brandt:** pp. iii, 88, 90 (all), 91, 92, 93; **Sheila Brislin:** p. 10; **Amy Carey:** p. 98; **Caters News Agency, Ltd.**—Martin Ellard: pp. ix (top), 182, 185, 186, 187, 188, 189; Luiz Higa Junior: p. vi; **Courtesy of Daniel Clarke:** pp. 82, 84, 85, 86 (all), 87; **Scott Cromwell:** pp. vii (left), x, 42, 45, 46, 47, 49; **Harold Daniels:** p. 69; **Courtesy of B. J. Duft:** p. 108; **Fame Pictures**—Barcroft Media: pp. 185, 161; **Julie Free:** pp. 216, 218, 219, 221; **Getty Images**—Barcroft: pp. viii (right), 146 (all), 149, 151, 190 (middle), 193, 194, 195 (top); Melanie Stetson Freeman/The Christian Science Monitor: pp. 94, 97 (top); David Silverman: pp. 126, 129; **Dave Hamman:** p. 200; **Courtesy of Rick Hamlin:** pp. 117, 118 (all); **Frank Hecker Naturfotografie:** pp. 130, 132, 133, 134, 136, 137; **Courtesy of Maureen Horgan:** p. 224; **IMP Features**—The Bui Sisters: pp. 174, 176, 179, 180, 181 (all); **Simon Jeffrey:** p. 231 (bottom); **Dr. Cynthia Jones:** pp. 70, 73; **Journal De Chambly**—Royal Adam: pp. 21, 22; Courtesy of Michelle Krawczyk: pp. 38 (all), 40; Morgan Brough p. 36; © **Joel Lemay/Agence QMI:** p. 18; **Courtesy of Colin and Theony MacRae:** p. 150; **Newspix**—Carly Earl pp. 12, 14, 15, 16, 17; **Newscom**—Albuquerque Journal/Zuma Press: pp. 103, 105, 107; Dan Callister/Pacific Coast News: p. 97 (left and bottom); **Courtesy of Oreo and Friends Animal Encounters:** pp. 190 (top and bottom); 192, 195 (bottom), 196 (all), 197; **Christie Pace:** pp. 52, 53, 55; **Courtesy of Mina and Michael Pinkston:** pp. ix (bottom), 114, 116, 119; **Reuters**—Rick Wilking: pp. 50, 57; **Rex**—Albanpix Ltd.: pp. 120 (all), 123; M & Y News Ltd: pp. 152, 155, 156, 157; Media Mode Pty Ltd: pp. 30, 33. 35; Les Wilson/Shutterstock: 228, 233; **Courtesy of Marcus Root:** pp. 58, 60, 62, 63 (all); **Rother Horsemanship:** pp. 162, 164; **Eden Hall:** pp. 166, 167; **SWNS.com:** pp. 231 (top), 232, 235; **Adam Gerrard:** pp. 76, 79, 81; **Fran Stothard:** pp. ix (2nd from top) 6, 8, 9, 11; **TheDobieTeam:** pp. ix (2nd from bottom), 204, 206, 208, 209; **Courtesy of Graham Waspe:** pp. 124, 125; **William Simmons Photography:** pp. 64, 66; **Courtesy of Warrnambool City Council:** pp. 108, 110, 111, 113; **Courtesy of Alicia Williams:** pp. 24, 26, 27, 28 (all), 29; **Courtesy of the Winokur Family:** p. 68; **Working Dogs for Conservation:** pp. 198, 203; **Courtesy of Taabish Zaver:** p. 168, 171.

Workman books are available at special discounts when purchased in bulk for premiums and sales promotions as well as for fund-raising or educational use. Special editions or book excerpts can also be created to specification. For details, contact the Special Sales Director at the address below, or send an email to specialmarkets@workman.com.

Workman Publishing Co., Inc.
225 Varick Street
New York, NY 10014-4381
workman.com

WORKMAN, UNLIKELY FRIENDSHIPS, and UNLIKELY LOVES
are registered trademarks of Workman Publishing Co., Inc.

Printed in China
First printing August 2016

10 9 8 7 6 5 4 3 2 1

For my adorably furry husband, John,
who loves dogs, too. (Honey, three is enough.)

Our Cover Dog

This is Bob. He is one of a pair of pups named after the music
legend Bob Marley, and he's about as smooth and easygoing as
his name suggests. (Turn on some reggae if you aren't sure what
I'm talking about.) This much loved golden retriever, who lives
in Brazil with owner Luiz, canine partner in sweetness Marley
(another golden), and a menagerie of little animals, is quite partial
to species that most dogs would treat as chew toys. He seems
most content—chin resting on the floor and tail flapping madly—
when surrounded by parakeets and finches and hamsters. As
one person posting on Bob's Facebook page noted, "Everybody
in Bob's world is always smiling! He brings such joy to so many
people and furry and feathered friends!"

"When the Man waked up he said,
'What is Wild Dog doing here?' And the Woman said,
'His name is not Wild Dog anymore, but the First Friend,
because he will be our friend for always
and always and always.'"

—RUDYARD KIPLING,
"The Cat That Walked by Himself"
(*Just So Stories*)

Contents

*Classic story from *Unlikely Friendships,
Unlikely Loves,* or *Unlikely Heroes.*

Introduction

WHAT IS IT ABOUT DOGS? WHETHER WE'RE OBSESSIVELY photographing them being adorable or boring friends at a party with "the hilarious thing my dog did" stories (guilty!), we can't seem to get enough of them. Their friendship with humans is certainly nothing new: Dogs were the first animals we domesticated—to me, one of our species' best accomplishments—and their bones mingle with ours in 12,000-year-old graves. The latest fossil discoveries suggest the line that led to our pets goes back more than 30,000 years, much further than previously thought.

We've been tweaking dogs to our liking ever since they joined our lives, fussing with size and color, with temperament and ability and looks, going from wolf to woof to yap and everything in between. Want a dog that fits in your purse? We've got those. Or one that can lead us to bad guys, bombs, and drugs? They're out there, too. There are the watchful and wary breeds, ready to leap to your defense, and the happy, lovable mutts with lolling tongues that ask only for a place in your lap and a kiss on the head. How wonderful that there are canines to suit each of us, to bring joy and, let's be honest, chaos to our lives.

Debates over dogs' origins have been fierce, and there's still no consensus about exactly when and where domestication happened. But *how* it happened may be a bit clearer. Many experts believe our bond with dogs began at the animals' initiation. Researchers theorize that wolves warily approached human settlements to pick at our food scraps, and with time, some were literally eating out of human hands. They even adapted to digesting the starchy foods that came from human agriculture; domestic dogs possess genes for that purpose that wolves don't have. With access to extra food, bold animals survived longer and bred more often than their cautious siblings. And so genes that made some of them "friendly" would have become more common, reinforcing the dog-human relationship.

Then, some of those same experts suggest, there may have come a second stage of domestication, when people, realizing the benefits of having canine companions as hunting buddies, actually captured wolf pups and raised them.

So, let's assume that dogs first sought out a partnership with people. Sure, that relationship was initially all about food, but what love affair doesn't start with a good meal? And now studies have shown that our love is mutual and has seeped all the way into our endocrine systems. When we gaze into the eyes of our furry friends, there is a rise in oxytocin—a hormone linked to trust and mother-infant bonds—both in their blood and in ours. We care about each other.

One reason early dogs thrived is because they gave back. While there's been a recent emphasis in the media on service dogs and how they benefit society, dogs actually have been serving us all along. For millennia, canines have been guards and hunters and sniffers on our behalf. They've rounded up our sheep and scared away predators from our villages and farms. They've carried messages and traveled with caravans and gone into battle with us. They've been our eyes and ears, our legs and noses, and even our hands when our own aren't working. And they've been devoted companions, forgiving us for our mistakes—even our cruelty—and loving us when we need it most.

In recent decades, the internet has given us a big shiny platform for showing off all the good stuff that dogs do. Scrolling through the endless postings of animal exploits (of which dogs are second only to cats in popularity—because, let's face it, cats are hilarious), we can't help but appreciate canines' openness toward others and willingness to help those in need. Sometimes dogs are simply more humane than humans are.

I love dogs. I suspect that's obvious from the books in this series. And when it comes to animal friendships, love, and heroism, dogs dominate. As much as I scour the animal kingdom to find the wacky and wonderful things other species are doing, *Canis lupus familiarus* is always just over my shoulder, stealing my attention with a tiny whimper and big sweet eyes.

And so, with this special volume, I'm giving in. Dogs, dogs, dogs! They're in every story, on every page. They pal around with other animals, showing how benevolent they can be, and they assist in all sorts of ways, from sniffing out a little girl's seizures to sticking by a trapped canine friend until a rescuer arrives. You'll also see included here some of the favorite and classic dog stories from the previous *Unlikely* books, but there is much fresh material, too, such as the mastiff who saved seventeen horses and a sweet pup with a chicken as a BFF. One doesn't have to look hard to find new cases of dogs showing empathy, kindness, or courage.

Necessarily, one book about dogs can only nibble at the edges of their generous offerings. With millions of pet pooches out there, how could we possibly keep up with so many memorable acts? They don't wait for us to hit "record" when they want to be awesome; they simply do their thing and then, easily distracted, rush headlong into something else.

Fortunately, we are together with dogs enough to witness a lot of behaviors worth our respect and even awe—and certainly our photos and videos. But more important, after such a long and ever-changing relationship with the human race, we're lucky that dogs still like having us around.

The author's beloved pups:
Monk (top, a Japanese Kai Ken),
Geddy (left, a Korean Jindo),
and Waits (also a Jindo).
Each is named after a musician.
All are spoiled beyond words.

The Junkyard Dog *and the* Goose

REX USED TO BE A JUNKYARD DOG. IT WASN'T ALL THAT long ago that this German shepherd—a breed often celebrated for its fine nose and police work—was pacing a chain-link fence, quick to growl, chase, or, if given the chance, bite anyone he didn't trust. And trust was not his strong point, for good reason. Rex's owner treated him terribly, ruling him with an iron fist (or in this case, an iron bar). Which explains why Rex became an animal as frightening as he was frightened, one whose future looked bleak.

Even after he was rescued by an animal welfare group and taken to a kennel, it was unclear what would happen to the beautiful but troubled pup. People generally don't adopt dogs that

One waddles, one trots.

bite. He was nearly put down for his horrendous manners.

But Rex's lousy luck took a very fortunate turn. Sheila Brislin, who runs another animal rescue facility, decided to bring Rex home and give him a better life. "The women caring for him at the dog pound showed me the bite marks all over their arms," she says. "Clearly they were very frightened of him." This didn't scare Sheila away. After hearing talk of the dog being put down, she says, "I sent my husband over to get Rex and bring him home."

With some twenty years of experience running the Puriton Horse and Animal Rescue in Somerset, England, Sheila wasn't one to give up on an animal, no matter how lost a cause it seemed. And she knew Rex was unlikely to be adopted as he was. "I could see he just needed support and love to get him to respect himself and others."

At home with Sheila and her family, Rex soon showed his aggressive nature, threatening to bite her son. "That was going to have to change quickly," Sheila says. "My husband grabbed him by the collar and shouted, 'Don't you dare bite us or you'll go back where you came from!' He used his voice to control Rex and it was quite effective."

A grooming session.

Both new dog and new owners had a lot to learn before they could trust one another. For example, "At first, when he misbehaved, we'd put him out on a chain," she says. "But then, we realized he was probably having flashbacks to his old life, to being tied out and beaten." They stopped chaining him up and things got better.

Still, Rex had a very strong prey drive, which was difficult to control. "We had lots of ducks and chickens and rabbits that we used to let roam free," Sheila says, "but with Rex around, we caged them for their own protection." It turned out to be an imperfect solution. "Rex would just put his head through the wire cage and bite them!"

BIG BITE

A German shepherd's jaw is a mighty thing, with some 240 pounds of force to its bite. A human jaw has less than 90 pounds.

Then Geraldine came to the farm. She was quite a bird, a very feisty goose—like Rex, perhaps a bit too feisty for some owners to handle. But not Sheila!

At first the goose ran around with some chickens, with Donald (a duck, of course),

A portrait-ready pair.

and with other avian sorts. Unfortunately, over time, she, too, showed a penchant for biting. She was the feathered Rex of the yard.

But then goose met dog. By mistake. "Gerry had gotten out of her area and Rex was there. We thought, *oh no, he's going to kill her!*"

No doubt it crossed Rex's mind to take a bite of the meaty bird. But Geraldine put a stop to that idea immediately. "She pecked him," Sheila recalls. Which might seem aggressive to us goose novices, but Sheila said it was more of a mothering peck. When she pecked him again, he seemed humbled somehow.

After the relatively smooth introduction, the two just started hanging around together, the goose pecking and grooming the dog, the dog licking the bird's face in return. The oddly matched animals were a couple. (A couple of what, it's hard to say!) They ate breakfast together, even sharing food (Geraldine took a liking to dog biscuits), and they slept in the dog bed in the kitchen, the goose tucked between Rex's paws.

Sheila says Rex was protective of his friend, even flinging a leg over her as they slept, and showed her a sweetness the owners didn't see otherwise: "He was such a softy around her." And the fondness went both ways: "If Rex had brambles or leaves stuck in his tail fur, Gerry would pull them out. It's hard to describe, but there was something in her face that showed she loved him. You never expect to see a goose acting so affectionately."

Unfortunately, Gerry passed away at the height of their relationship, and the dog took it hard. "Rex is more loving [toward us] but seems lost without her," says Sheila. "We now have eight new geese, and when they arrived, he ran over to meet them. But [after he checked them out] he turned and sat down and lowered his head. He must really miss his friend."

But Rex and Gerry certainly made the most of that year and a half they spent together. The dog and the goose were virtually inseparable. Even when the family went to the beach or the woods for a walk with Rex, Sheila says, "Gerry would not be left behind! It was a wonderful surprise to see them find friendship." They were two of a kind and they were completely different. The way friends should be.

The Bernese Mountain Dog and the Ferret

IN THIS WILD AND WACKY WORLD OF OURS, IT CAN BE HARD to find balance in one's life.

Well, here are two animals who have done just that—by being together. One towers above, one skitters below. One is mellow and tangle-haired, the other nervous and neat. Each is what the other isn't, and that makes them the perfect pair.

Let's start with Mischka, a 90-pound Bernese mountain dog who's mild-mannered and sweet, all big paws and "come play with me" eyes, who waits for her pal each day like a lovesick teenager by the phone. And then there's little Jerry, the ferret, a bit tubby for his kind, but still speedy and delightfully wiggly, seemingly always on his way to do something very important. It would take

The owners with their pets.

forty Jerries to make a Mischka. That means just one wrong step by Mischka could mean one very bad day for Jerry. "If she plunked a foot squarely on him," says the dog's owner, Christine Woodward, "she'd crush him!"

But these two know how to handle each other: Mischka is gentle with her little friend, and Jerry seems to know just how much high-energy ferret time the dog will tolerate. (A lot.) Though a ferret may sleep 20 hours a day, "so soundly you might think it has died," says Jerry's owner, Susan Mitchell, "when he's awake, it's like flipping a switch—he is totally on." So it's a good thing that, despite her imposing size, Mischka is so tolerant and patient. "She lets Jerry climb all over her," says Christine.

How did the two meet? In the way neighbors often do, over—or, in this case, under—a fence. Susan regularly walks Jerry, strapped into a little harness, through their neighborhood in suburban Sydney, Australia. On one of those walks, her pet's snout started vibrating as he drew near a yard where a striking tri-colored dog stood watching. The two curious creatures went nose to nose, trying to figure each other out. The result was clear: "They had an instant bond," says Christine.

And now when Mischka hears the jingle of the little bell Jerry wears on his collar, she goes to the door barking, wanting to greet her friend. Their playing style isn't quite dog and isn't quite ferret, but something they've invented. (Mischka has tried to find Jerry's inner dog, nudging her toys in front of his face, but Jerry has never quite known what to do with them.)

Picture this: Jerry pokes around in one of Mischka's ears— following a scent, nibbling on an itch—and when the dog turns her head, he works on the other. When Mischka lies down and gives Jerry full access to her glorious coat, he searches out the coziest, furriest spot and burrows underneath. "I've learned that ferrets love nuzzling into warm places," Christine says.

Sometimes Jerry goes off on his own, as ferrets will do, investigating spaces too small even for Mischka's muzzle. "Ferrets are busy and curious like kittens," Susan explains. So when Jerry is feeling independent, the dog tails her friend, watching him squirm in and out of boxes, and over and under cushions, waiting for his attention to turn back her way.

Sometimes she nudges for that attention with an outstretched paw. But she's always careful. "She doesn't quite touch him, or she touches very gently, as if

she knows she could hurt him," Christine says. Even though Bernese mountain dogs are known to stay puppylike for longer than most breeds, Mischka doesn't fling herself around willy-nilly like a youngster. "She never gets too boisterous, not the way she will with another dog," Christine says.

Which is good, because an annoyed ferret may bite. Susan isn't too worried about this happening with Jerry, though. She says he's particularly tender compared with some other ferrets she's known. Still, in this relationship, it seems that Jerry sets the tone, and Mischka is happy to let him. It's in her nature, after all: Bernese mountain dogs are known for taking direction well. They were bred for draft work, meaning Mischka could easily be trained to pull a wagon. What a scene that would be, Jerry riding in high style behind his loyal hauler. Talk about a sweet ride!

Susan has had many ferrets as pets over the years, as many as four at a time. She can tell you all kinds of surprising facts about the animals, which in some countries are nearly as popular pets as cats and dogs are in the United States. "They're not rodents," Susan points out, which is a common misconception. They are a domesticated form of the European polecat, close kin to weasels, otters, and badgers.

Right now, Susan has just two—Jerry and another ferret called Honey, and they get along fine. But when it comes to a best friend, the little ferret's heart lies with the big dog, and together, the pair warms the hearts of everyone in the neighborhood. "As you can imagine," says Christine, "when they're out in the garden together, with Mischka standing tall over Jerry and Jerry looking up at Mischka, they attract quite a bit of attention."

The proud owner and his hero.

The Mastiff Who Saved Seventeen Horses

POPEYE IS AN **I**TALIAN MASTIFF—ALSO CALLED A **C**ANE Corso. Without knowing anything in particular about him, you can't help but be wowed by this dignified giant. His imposing head wears a silky gray hood that ends in floppy, frowning lips and a dangling wattle, like a handkerchief drooping from his neck. His eyes are watery and deep, as if he's grown weary of a world that doesn't quite meet his high standards. A top hat and monocle would suit him.

Words often applied to mastiffs—watchful, majestic, intelligent, loyal—describe this dog perfectly. Popeye proved himself on every count in the middle of the night on October 8, 2013, when a fire broke out at his master's Montreal equestrian center.

If you ask Gilles Godbout what his seven-year-old dog did on that desperate night, the man gets a little weepy. If it weren't for Popeye, he says, he's not sure where he'd be today.

He recalls waking around 3 a.m., sensing something was wrong. "Out the window of my bedroom, I could see a reddish light, a glow. When I looked out I could see my barn burning. And the first thing I said to my wife was, 'I have to save the horses!'"

Horses are Gilles's life. By that point, he'd been training them for some thirty years, and riding and showing even longer. "My grandfather was a farrier [a blacksmith who shoes horses], so I learned a lot about horses from him," he says. After two decades working at other stables, in 2008 he bought a farm and opened his own equestrian center. At the time of the fire, he had a full house, with thirty-one horses occupying his stalls.

When he saw the flames licking the stable roof, Gilles raced to the barn to try to free his horses. "It was a really dark night, and there was so much heat and smoke, it was hard to see what I was doing." It took him at least five minutes just to coax the first horse out, and he quickly realized he was facing tragedy. "Horses have a specific reaction to fire; they want to stay in the stall," he says. "They're afraid to move." He feared he'd lose all the rest.

Popeye always followed his master's lead. The dog was ever present in the arena during classes and horse shows, always a

The 2013 fire quickly consumed Gilles's barn.

part of everything that went on at the center. And, says Gilles, he was always watchful of his owner and of the horses, especially the young, nervous ones, like a big brother keeping his eye on his little (or, in this case, not so little) siblings.

This night was no exception. "Popeye was there, right by my side, and he checked my eyes, as if he was waiting for my command," Gilles says. "I could tell he knew how bad things were and wanted to do something. So I opened the next stall and told him, 'Yes, you can help me! Go!'"

Popeye didn't hesitate. "He ran into the stall and began nipping at the legs of the horse," which got it moving. Then he returned to Gilles, again watching his face. Gilles quickly opened

Safe from the fire.

the next door, and Popeye repeated the effort, rushing in, biting legs, and chasing the horse out. In this way, in just about five minutes—the time it had taken Gilles to rescue a single animal—Popeye got seventeen horses out of the stable and onto safe ground.

The last horse to escape the blaze "came out with his mane on fire," Gilles says. Moments earlier, "the roof had begun to cave in, and a fireman grabbed me to hold me back. But Popeye bolted in anyway." Fortunately, the horse made it out before the roof collapsed, with Popeye nipping at its hooves.

"Popeye did what he had to do to save the animals," Gilles marvels. "He burned his paws a little but that didn't stop him."

Three of the horses had bolted as they left the barn. Later, Popeye went out and rounded them up—after the firemen had no luck getting them to turn back. "The horses knew Popeye. They trusted him. It was as if my dog knew the job wasn't done. He had to complete the rescue," Gilles says.

Not long after the fire, with TV cameras rolling, Popeye was given an award for his bravery by the Quebec Association for Veterinarians. The huge mastiff lay calmly on stage as Gilles recounted his amazing behavior. And in 2014, Gilles managed to rebuild his stable and get his business up and running again.

Though thirteen horses died in the blaze—a massive emotional and financial loss—the seventeen animals Popeye saved (plus the one that Gilles rescued) were enough to keep him going.

Says Gilles, "Popeye knows horses better than most people do, and he knew what to do that night, how to save them. He would have given his life for them. I owe him so much."

He speaks with love and pride not just about the dog's heroics, but about Popeye's commitment to him and the other animals. "He's more than a pet; he's a real friend and partner to me. We are always on the job together. He's one very special dog."

The modest hero at rest.

The Two-Wheeled Chihuahua *and the* Silkie Chicken

AS THE OWNER OF THREE DOGS, I SPEND PLENTY OF time in the waiting room at the veterinary clinic. I see a lot of other dogs there, as you might expect. There are usually a couple of cats, too, tucked into crates, making their dissatisfaction heard.

What I've never seen at my vet's office is a chicken. But at the Duluth Animal Hospital in Georgia, one chicken is a regular. Her name is Penny. At first glance, you might not know she *is* a chicken—she's no chin-jutting barnyard clucker, but a precious ball of white fluff. A marshmallow. A shmoo. If you were to groom a white alpaca, you could make a Penny look-alike from what comes off the brush. The only real sign she's a bird is a tiny beak poking out from what must be her head. Even her knobby little bird feet

are tucked inside plush winter slippers. She's really all feather and no peck.

Penny is a breed of chicken called a Silkie—the perfect name. Silkies originated in China but nowadays they are raised all over. They're unique not just for their luxurious and soft plumage (which isn't always white) but for really weird hidden traits like black skin and bones and blue earlobes. (Really!)

Clearly, Penny isn't your average bird, so I guess it shouldn't be surprising that she chose an atypical best friend. Her BFF is Roo, a two-legged, two-wheeled Chihuahua. Roo was six weeks old when he was rescued from a drainage ditch and brought to the animal hospital. "One of our clients saw the grass moving and went to investigate; that's the only reason Roo was discovered," says Alicia Williams, who works in client services at the hospital. The little guy was missing his front legs (and some teeth); he appeared to have been born that way.

To Alicia, these genetic anomalies only added to his charm. She took Roo home that night and has been his loving mom ever since. Eventually, thanks to a generous benefactor who also fell in love with the little dog, Roo was outfitted with his own special wagon, which lets him wheel around at top speed. He's had some knee issues since then, but after surgery and hydrotherapy (yes, the pampered Chihuahua does his exercises in a pool), he continues to get around just fine.

Alicia had adopted Penny not long before Roo, from a scientific laboratory. She knew nothing about chickens except that she wanted to save this one from its unhappy fate. And she never regretted her decision. "People often assume chickens aren't intelligent, but she knows her name and comes running to me like a dog," Alicia says. "She has favorite foods, favorite people." Penny hadn't gotten affection from people before Alicia came along, and it took a little time for her to learn trust, "but now she'll sit on your lap, purr, and talk to you."

The first interaction between Roo and the now-gregarious chicken was a good sign of the friendship to come. "I had set up a bed for Roo, and when I put him in it, Penny came over to check him out," Alicia recalls. "He tried to play, pulling at her feathers, and she was tolerant. And then when he fell asleep, she climbed on top of him like he was her egg."

Friends for all seasons . . .

Now they spend nearly all their time together. Alicia brings them to work—both are social animals, after all, and seem to love the noise and activity of the clinic. Not surprising, they're a big hit there, with Roo zooming through the reception area on his wheels and Penny wandering around in her "chicken diaper." (Yes, it's for what you think.) The animals have also been known to dress up, even wearing matching tutus, and seem to love kids, a fondness that goes both ways, of course.

Roo is now a few pounds heavier than his fluffy companion, but Penny still climbs on him like he's hers to keep warm and safe. She loves nuzzling the pup, preening him as she would her own chick. And occasionally, she'll do something wonderfully peculiar: She'll lay an egg in the bed where they first met and leave it there for Roo to find. What the Chihuahua makes of this strange gift is a mystery, but he gently nestles beside it, treating it like a little treasure. Perhaps he knows it's a gesture of love from his special friend.

The
Spotted Lamb
and the Dalmatian

FIRST OF ALL, LET'S DISPEL THE RUMORS, SHALL WE? No, a ram did not mate with a dalmatian to produce Lambie, the remarkably dalmatianlike lamb in this story. (Come on, the thought did cross your mind, didn't it?) Nature doesn't work that way. Dogs and sheep may show affection for each other, but they don't make babies together.

Still, the coincidence, call it biological serendipity, was awesome.

Julie Bolton of South Adelaide, Australia, breeds dalmatians, including seven-year-old Zoe, a gorgeous champion in the dog-show world. She's also a take-charge kind of animal, her owner says. In her own litter, "she was the first one out, and she made eye contact with me first—she was just a little more forward than the others." That forwardness even translates to her breeding schedule; she comes into heat (is ready to mate) regularly before the other female dogs, as if to prove she's number one. She also happens to be a very good mother.

Julie and her family keep other animals besides dogs on their 32-acre Australian homestead. Sheep included. One day, one of the female sheep (called a ewe) gave birth to a tiny lamb that looked more like a spotted puppy than a sheep-to-be. The ewe took one look at the slippery runt on the ground and ran to the other side of the paddock, utterly uninterested in doing her motherly duties. (Almost certainly, the lamb's looks had nothing to do with her being abandoned; sheep focus more on smells and sounds when it comes to recognizing their young.)

Though she wasn't thrilled to have an orphan lamb on her hands, Julie couldn't help but laugh at the strangeness of the situation: "a lamb like a spotted puppy born in a home full of dalmatians," she says. "It was a lovely surprise."

And the story gets better. With the lamb left parentless, "Zoe immediately went to it, drawn by that newborn smell," Julie says. "And she started to lick it, automatically doing what the mother would do." Meanwhile, the lamb-that-looked-like-a-dalmatian-puppy wanted milk and was looking for its mother. "Normally, mother sheep will make an *eeeee* sound and the baby will reply with an *eeeeee*, which helps mothers know whose baby is whose in a flock," Julie explains.

But this lamb's mom made no noise; she had zero motherly know-how. So the lamb transferred its own instinctive behavior onto Zoe. The shape and size of the animal was close enough, so Lambie went for where the udder would be, head butting, looking for a drink. Zoe, without milk at the time, turned and nuzzled it, Julie recalls. "I fed the lamb with a bottle and Zoe stayed there with me, cleaning it up. Very motherly."

Although Julie continued with the feeding duties by bottle, the bond between the two spotted creatures was set. "It was instant love that day," Julie recalls, and if Zoe could have fed Lambie herself, no doubt she would have. The abandoned lamb thrived only because Zoe was there to fill in for the ewe. "Lambie has never been sick, has always eaten well, has never acted depressed," Julie says. "For its health, that psychological and physical connection was so important. If you put a lamb by itself, it won't be as robust."

With time, Lambie has become more independent, eating grass out in the sunshine and doing lamb things, and even its coloration has changed to where it is less spotted than before. But when Julie takes Zoe for a walk, the lamb trots along with them, sometimes tapping its nose to the back of Julie's or Zoe's legs as it would to keep from getting separated from its mother in the tall grass. And other times, it runs

DOGGY DUTIES

According to the American Kennel Club, the dog we know as the dalmatian has played many roles over its history, including that of dog of war, draft dog, shepherd, ratter, firehouse mascot, bird dog, trail hound, and accomplished retriever. Most significant, it is the first and only coach dog—guardian of the horse-drawn carriage.

along full of joy, like a gazelle with all four feet coming off the ground, what Julie calls "the Lamb Olympics." Zoe and some of the other dogs will play with Lambie when the animal is in such an exuberant mood, but they are gentle with the unique baby.

As Julie reminds us, the lamb turning to Zoe when the ewe bolted was simply instinct. "Survival, you see. A baby needs to find milk. If it had seen a pig moving around," she says, "it would have bonded with the pig." A lamb needs two things, food and the flock, she says, and will seek those things in whatever animal is present. It didn't have to be Zoe.

But in this case, the little spotted lamb happened to bond with the big spotted dalmatian. And that makes this love story perfectly delightful.

The Little Girl and Her Guardian Angel

IN A HOSPITAL ROOM IN NORTH CAROLINA, A WISP OF A girl named Kaelyn Krawczyk (called KK) is curled up in bed in her favorite pink polka-dotted pajamas. But she's not alone—a beloved pal is tucked in next to her. The bedmate is white and hairy, with a cold nose and soulful eyes. Her name is JJ, and she's not just Kaelyn's pet pup. She's her most loyal friend and her protector. Lifesaver, even.

Here is a child, still a customer of the tooth fairy, who has already been through more hard times than most of us experience in our whole lives. She has a rare disease called mastocytosis, which occurs when the body produces too many mast cells (part of the immune system). Mast cell overproduction can lead to symptoms

Hospital stays are better with a friend.

like rashes, stomach and bone pain, infections, and, most dangerous, anaphylaxis, which is a severe allergic reaction that can send the body into shock or even be fatal.

On a good day, KK takes eleven pills, and she's not supposed to play tag or climb trees or ice skate—in fact, she has to avoid pretty much anything that might make her hot, cold, tired, or excited. Whatever revs her up or wears her out can make her very sick. The hospital is familiar territory, and these days, she has to be homeschooled because her fragility is too much for public schools to handle. Mastocytosis makes it really hard to be a kid.

But if you ask KK how she feels about missing out on all that fun stuff, she's likely to tell you it's not so bad, that actually she's lucky—because she gets to spend all her time with her remarkable and adoring dog.

The pup, who by happy chance was already named JJ when

she moved in with the Krawczyk family, is so connected to KK that during surgery a couple of years back, she was allowed in the operating room. It wasn't just the patient who wanted her to be there, but the doctors, too. "They've realized that JJ is better at monitoring Kaelyn's health than even the most modern medical machines," says Michelle, KK's mom.

What JJ can do is truly remarkable. She knows when her girl needs help, by a change in scent and perhaps other subtle signals—such as a drop in blood pressure or heart rate or a change in body temperature—even before KK's symptoms are obvious. She'll alert others, by barking, pawing an adult, or fetching the kit with KK's medicine, enough in advance that they can stop the reaction before it gets more serious.

During one hospital stay, JJ escaped her crate and ran down the hall to alert Michelle (who was speaking with nurses) that the patient was in trouble. This was before the monitors registered a change in Kaelyn's vital signs, which they did moments later. "JJ knew something was wrong before it actually occurred. That let the docs and nurses know to trust this dog," says Michelle.

How did JJ become Kaelyn's friend and protector? "We had just found out from the allergist that it wasn't safe for KK to attend school, which was devastating," Michelle recalls. "My husband, John, and I were sitting together with our goldendoodle [a golden retriever crossed with a poodle], who was resting his head in my husband's lap. John sighed and said to him, 'If only you could go to school and watch over KK.'"

KK reads to her pup.

Michelle thought, *Why not get a dog to watch over our daughter? Maybe one could be trained to alert us if KK falls, or if her blood pressure is low, or if she loses consciousness—things that concern us all the time.* For years, Kaelyn's parents had been checking on their daughter throughout the night, and their anxiety was no less during the day. With so many triggers for dangerous symptoms, keeping tabs on KK was a full-time, and emotionally consuming, job. Imagine the relief if they could know their little girl was being carefully monitored all the time—that she was in very good . . . paws?

Michelle did some research, but it wasn't easy to find a service dog trained specifically for someone with mastocytosis. She finally located a trainer willing to help: Deb Cunningham, whom Michelle found though a nonprofit called Eyes, Ears, Nose, and Paws. Deb tested whether the disease offered up a unique scent that a dog could detect, using clothes that KK and other mastocytosis sufferers had worn during reactions. And she found that there *was* a telltale odor that a dog could identify.

And then came the real test. "We were at an open house at the dog-training center," Michelle says. KK started feeling poorly, so Deb cleared the other that dogs out of the room and brought JJ to the child. "Deb said, 'Smell it,' and JJ went crazy!" Michelle recalls. "The dog started alerting, then rushed to get the medical kit, as she'd been trained to do. But instead of giving it to Deb, she brought it to me—even though we'd only met briefly. Somehow, she knew I was in charge of KK and wanted me to help her."

Since then, the little white mutt has been glued to her young charge and absolutely on target with her alerts—which happen just about every day for mild symptoms and, because of the dog's early warnings, fewer than once a year for severe ones. (ER visits are much rarer nowadays.) JJ's careful monitoring has even allowed KK to try many more "high-risk" activities (normal kid stuff) without her parents worrying.

"There's no doubt in my mind that JJ knows her job is to keep KK safe," her mom says. And just as clear is how much Kaelyn appreciates and adores JJ. "She snuggles me, she keeps me safe, plus she's really cute," the little girl says. KK's word for how big her love is for JJ? "A fillion"—way more than a million or a billion, obviously.

Michelle points to a special moment that seems to sum it all up. "KK's kindergarten teacher [before homeschooling began] asked her to draw a self-portrait. She explained that that meant it should just be KK in the picture, not her whole family." So KK drew herself. But then she drew JJ by her side. "To her, they are one."

TRICKY ILLNESS

A person with mastocytosis may react to foods, certain types of weather, sunlight, exercise, perfume, or insect bites. Medication, too, can trigger a bad reaction, making it very hard to treat the symptoms and risky to do surgery.

Winston with Kammer.

The Chameleon *and* *the* Yellow Lab

IUSED TO HAVE A LITTLE CHAMELEON NAMED **HANK. ONE** day he escaped. Without the safety—and moist heat—of his tank, I figured he'd soon be a little of pile of bones behind a dresser.

Instead, Tai, one of my dogs, saved his little life. She found him and gently carried him around in her warm, wet mouth, then returned him to me, alive and kicking. A dog saving a reptile. What a strange interspecies rescue!

Though not a rescue operation, I couldn't help but think about Tai and Hank when I saw photos of Winston the yellow lab posing with Kammer and, in other photos, Geoffrey—both panther chameleons. Just look at these photos and try not to smile: Kammer balances on the dog's head. Geoffrey reaches toward the dog with one alien hand as if to scratch his chin. Kammer, with Winston as audience, snaps up a worm or bit of fruit offered by his owner. (Rarely are there leftovers for the dog, but he stands ready, just in case.) Oklahoman Scott Cromwell, when not working as a TV repairman (probably one of the last few on Earth, he jokes), shoots photos of his menagerie performing their weird, colorful theater.

Panther chameleons, native to Madagascar, are giants compared with my Hank, who was a different species. But they all share the cool chameleon characteristics, such as cone-shaped eyes that swivel independently, skin that changes colors (in response to light, temperature, and emotional state), and a prehensile tail—sort of a "fifth hand" that hangs on tight even when the other hands are busy. Other than their rapid-fire tongues, the reptiles often move at sloth speed, slowly rocking forward and back, forward and back, arm outstretched, perpetually

For Kammer, nabbing a snack requires a rocket-fast tongue and a patient dog.

undecided about taking a step. They're sort of the opposite of your friendly neighborhood lab, who is likely to race ahead unguarded and unwilling to miss a thing. (Winston has better manners than some labs, but he's still a dog, prone to dog excitement and impulsive forward motion.)

Though both of Scott's chameleons know Winston, Kammer is the one who might call the yellow dog a friend.

Winston is "a super-cool, laid-back dog," says Scott, who got the lab as a six-week-old pup six years ago. He puts up with whatever comes his way, adopting the relaxed attitude of his owner. This demeanor comes in handy when he's got a 1½-foot-long chameleon perched on his bony head—Scott's favorite position to photograph.

Geoffrey was the first chameleon in the family and so the first to interact with Winston. He had no fear of the big dog—which gave Scott the idea to set up the funny portraits. Pairing up such disparate animals was good fun, plus it seemed to entertain Winston better than some of his toys. Still, there didn't seem to be much going on between the two animals. They were both just . . . there.

Winston with Geoffrey.

But then Scott brought Kammer home, and as he watched the new chameleon check out Winston, he realized there was something a little like friendship in the making. On their first meeting, he recalls, "Winston was just lying on the bed and Kammer went right up to him. There was no

Another shot at lunch.

animosity, no fear—they were fine right off the bat. They seemed curious about each other, that's all." While some dogs would back away from, bark at, or swipe a paw at such an interloper in his territory, Winston did none of those things. He was all nose, sniffing, sniffing, probably realizing (as dogs have amazingly sensitive noses) this familiar creature was not the one he'd sniffed before. And he seemed happy with the change.

Really, any show of welcome on the reptile's part would be surprising. "Mostly chameleons aren't particularly friendly; they don't really want to be handled or bothered," Scott says. A chameleon's mad hiss can be quite intimidating. But after having Kammer just a short time, Scott noticed that he actually sought out attention: "When he saw me come in the room, he'd run to the front of his cage wanting to come out. And now he does that when he sees Winston, too." If Winston is curled up on the bed or sprawled on the floor and Scott lets Kammer out, "he goes right over to the dog, maybe even climbs over his leg," Scott says, and hangs out right there with him. They'll eat together, too. And of course, there's the time spent atop Winston's head or back. As much as a chameleon can be a friend to another animal, Kammer seems to be trying his best.

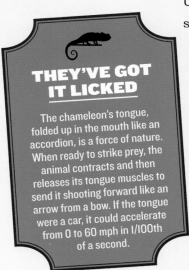

THEY'VE GOT IT LICKED

The chameleon's tongue, folded up in the mouth like an accordion, is a force of nature. When ready to strike prey, the animal contracts and then releases its tongue muscles to send it shooting forward like an arrow from a bow. If the tongue were a car, it could accelerate from 0 to 60 mph in 1/100th of a second.

Unlike your favorite furry mammal friendships, these two don't cuddle up for naps or wrestle around the living room. The dog might occasionally lick his scaly pal, but Kammer offers no return kiss. If you've ever watched a chameleon eat, you'd realize why not. This animal's tongue, which usually sits rolled up in its mouth, is a muscular cylinder that can unfurl to 1½ times the chameleon's body length—so fast you'll miss it if you blink. Someone measured and reported that the tongue actually accelerates five times faster than an F16 fighter jet! And it's sticky on the end. That's a tool made not for gentle and steady licking but for nabbing an insect and yanking it back into the mouth. Nature is quite the engineer!

Still, even without the typical affectionate displays, for a couple of hours to a full day at a time (when Kammer is given the run of the house), the chameleon and dog spend quality time

Dining together (on different foods).

together, socializing in their own unique way. They're sort of like two old men who meet daily on a park bench, each thinking his own thoughts but enjoying the other's company, now and then leaning close to exchange a word or two. They're quiet companions with something unspoken in common.

Meanwhile, the funny pair has given the man behind the camera some truly unique tableaux—and a memorable way to spend his Sunday afternoons.

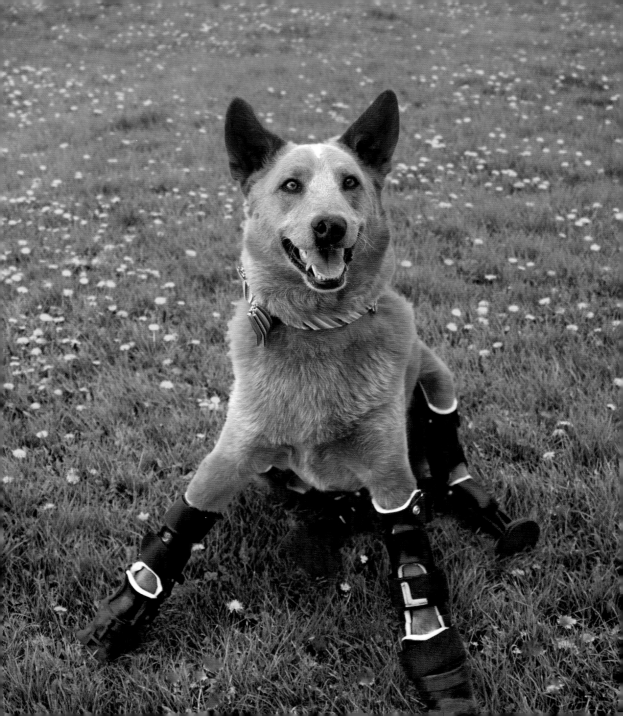

The
Bionic
Dog

"THERE'S A BIT OF MAGIC IN EVERYTHING, AND SOME loss to even things out."** It's a line from a Lou Reed song, and it makes me think about a sweet pup named Naki'o. In Naki'o's case, first came a lot of loss, then just the right amount of magic. Loss returned briefly, then the magic swooped back in. And through it all, this dog held on to his joyous and heroic spirit.

As a tiny puppy back in 2010, Naki'o was discovered with his family in the ice-cold basement of a Nebraska home. The owners had fled foreclosure, and their dog was left behind either pregnant or having recently given birth. The mama didn't survive, but when rescuers arrived they found her puppies—red heeler mixed breeds—miraculously still alive and squirming. One of them, though, was in very rough shape, severely frostbitten, his paws held fast to a frozen puddle on the basement floor.

All four feet had to be amputated to save this little dog's life. For an animal built to run and play, such a loss could have been devastating, and might have made the dog undesirable to potential adoptive parents. But then came the first spark of magic.

Christie Pace was scrolling through a pet-finding website when she came across Stubby (as he was then known) and his sad story. "That day, I was really just perusing to get an idea

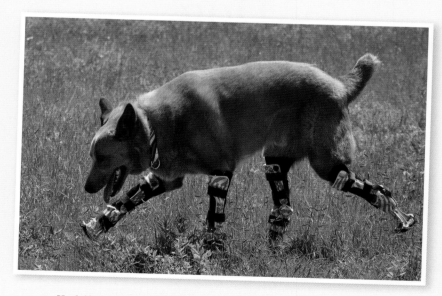

Naki'o's prosthetics are decorated in American flags to pay tribute to veteran amputees.

Naki'o inspires other disabled pets.

of what kind of dog I might want to adopt, not to actually pick one." But when she saw the photo and read Stubby's history, she says, "I fell in love. I went to see him, and he was all smiles, running on his little stumps and jumping into my lap to kiss me." The dog had also lost a bit of his tail, a nip of nose, and a chunk of ear from the frostbite, but somehow these scars added to his charm. "Of course," says Christie, "I brought him home."

That Stubby was a special-needs dog didn't worry Christie, who was a veterinary technician and was allowed to take him to work with her each day. Plus, he was so joyful, so seemingly unaware of his missing feet, and able to maneuver pretty darn well without them. One leg was worse than the others, and Christie thought she might have to address it down the line. But for the time being, both she and the dog managed.

As Stubby—whom Christie renamed Naki'o, meaning "puddle" in Hawaiian—grew and his bones took shape, he began to struggle with his disability. (The dog's new name reflected his birthplace, the cause of the pup's injuries, and his "mistakes"

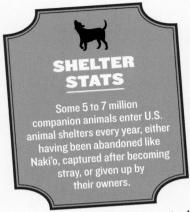

SHELTER STATS

Some 5 to 7 million companion animals enter U.S. animal shelters every year, either having been abandoned like Naki'o, captured after becoming stray, or given up by their owners.

during house training.) He also got heavier. "I had to carry him everywhere, put him in the car, help him up the steps," Christie says. "We couldn't really take a walk, and if he was out to play, he had to stay on the soft grass. Carrying him was fine when he was little, but by the time he was fifty pounds, it was pretty difficult!" Christie used a stroller and a red wagon to help cart the pup around, but it was slow going.

"He didn't like to be left at home. He wanted to be involved with the family all the time."

Still, "he never complained," Christie marvels. "His personality was still great, he was always happy. But there were little signs, behaviors, showing that he was in pain." And soon that pain turned to sores on the most damaged back leg, which Christie worried could become infected. "It was a constant battle with antibiotics, pain medications. We were always soaking his sores, trying to heal them." When Naki'o was one year old and still struggling, she knew it was time to try something new.

Christie began researching prosthetics. She heard of a company called OrthoPets that makes custom prosthetics for animals with great success. "It was fate," she says. "They were exactly what I needed. It was a blessing that I came across them."

Raising $1,000 for the first leg was easy. "We put a jar up front at the vet clinic and lots of clients donated. They all knew Naki'o, knew his story, and they'd bonded with him at the clinic. The

community really pulled together."
Then OrthoPets did a wonderful
thing: The company donated the
other three prosthetics!

The hind leg prosthetics
were made first, one at a time,
and Naki'o pretty quickly figured out how to walk around on
them. "He became comfortable,"
Christie remembers, "and was
able to play outside and chase
balls with less pain."

Staying fit with hydrotherapy.

With that victory, OrthoPets suggested doing both front paws
at once, to even him out.

The procedure goes like this: First, vets do a simple surgery
on each leg to clean and smooth the surface of the bone where
the prosthetic will go. Then the new legs are cast, with lots of
cushioning, to fit the leg nubs perfectly. Each leg nub goes into a
socket that closes on it like a clamshell while letting the animal's
knee bend above it. Velcro straps and padding hold it in place. The
"feet" don't resemble animal paws—the black rubber-bottomed
parts seem more apt for a table than a dog, but they hold up to
romps and leaps as well as any natural body part does.

And suddenly, the dog with no feet had four on the floor.

"The first time he stood up he was wobbly, like a newborn
fawn. Having had no paws, he didn't know where his limbs were

in space." But then, says Christie, "he started walking, then running and jumping. He was doing everything he couldn't do before, and loving it. We'd actually take a real walk down the street! That was a great accomplishment, and of course everyone stopped to meet him."

Since rising to the occasion, Naki'o not only gets excited when he sees his prosthetic legs (like some dogs respond when the leash comes out), but he has become even more confident and even friendlier than he was before . . . and that's saying a lot. Christie says, "He's so good with all kinds of people—children, elderly—and with other animals. I know it's because of what he's gone through."

His original prosthetics have been tweaked and reworked over time for an even better fit. And Christie selected a very special design to decorate them. "I picked the American flag. There were lots of options—camouflage and flowers and such. But I like the flag, because I think of him as a hero and wanted to pay tribute to him and to the war-hero amputees who have struggled like he has. To say thank you."

Naki'o's ease and sweet temperament despite his ordeal have brought him much attention. "People see how much I've done for him, but really what's important is how much he's doing for others. How happy he is—how much joy and spirit and life he has—sets such a positive example. He's educating people that animals with serious disabilities can have a great quality of life."

And this "silly boy," as she calls him, seems to love showing off his newly found abilities. He's participated in an agility course—through tunnels, up A-frames, between poles. "If anyone doubted he could do it, he certainly showed them!" Christie recalls with pride. She's taken him to rallies for disabled pets and to visit kids with disabilities. And most important, he inspired Christie to found a rescue organization in his name. Through Naki'o's Underdog Rescue, in Colorado Springs, Christie has been helping dogs and cats with disabilities to find loving homes. She's even had a few come in from overseas.

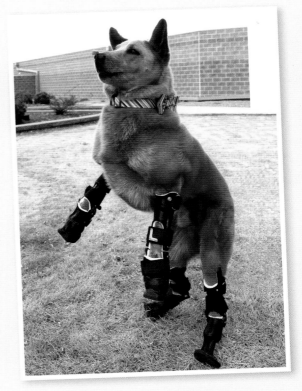

With his new legs, Naki'o can run, jump, and stand tall.

"We may not be able to assist animals in huge volume, but the few disabled animals we can help are worth it all," she says.

Meanwhile, Naki'o, unaware of the hero within him, keeps kicking up those feet and making people smile, bringing a little bit of magic wherever his new legs carry him.

The body language of play crosses species.

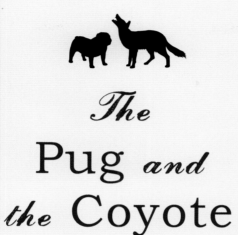

The
Pug *and*
the Coyote

WHAT DO WE THINK OF WHEN WE THINK OF COYOTES? Perhaps the trademark howl comes to mind, or a certain famous cartoon character falling yet again off a cliff in pursuit of a very speedy bird. But after that, the coyote reputation gets a bit dodgy. Skulking, skinny, and in need of a good scubbing. Always at the margins, looking for a way in. Pet snatcher.

But it's important to challenge assumptions. And coyotes are, if you give them a chance, beautiful and fascinating animals. When coyotes kill pets, it's because they're hungry and because people (and their pets) have intruded on their natural habitat, making wild prey more scarce. True, they are opportunistic—meaning they'll take easy prey (a chubby house cat), and if some other hunter

does the work of bring-
ing down dinner, they're
happy to snag a bite of
the spoils. It may seem
disreputable to us, but
from the coyote's per-
spective, it's just a good
survival strategy.

But here's a coyote
that has beaten back
stereotypes and shown
excellent manners. Rather than turn a small dog into dinner, it
befriended him. And this wasn't a dog that could have passed for
even a distant relative of the coyote. We're talking a smush-faced,
sausage-shaped, snorting little pug. (No offense to pugs. That's just
how they are—and we love them for it.) A creature invented by dog
breeders, not domesticated from wild stock. Somehow, that makes
the friendship between these two all the more extraordinary.

Tucked away in the city of Gilbert, Arizona, is a 110-acre
park of marshland, lakes, ponds, and gardens called the Gilbert
Riparian Preserve. Set up with water recycling and conservation
in mind, it's also a haven for hikers (and their dogs) and all kinds
of wildlife. Including coyotes.

Marcus Root walks in the preserve often. And he always
takes his pug, Harvey, who seems to love the place as much as
his owner does.

Marcus's wife, Jinia, had brought the pug home a couple of years before. The wee pup won her over despite being the total opposite of her previous dog, a mastiff, who had recently died. "Puppies make everything better," Jinia says. "And you know how you see dogs that stay by their owner's side and sit still when other dogs walk by? We'd been waiting for a dog like that. And now we have that in Harvey."

Marcus might have been briefly irritated at his wife for bringing home a new pup without his input, but the curious, energetic little dog soon had him smitten, too. "And now, it's mostly my husband who takes Harvey out and hikes with him. They have such a great friendship," Jinia says.

It was on one of those hikes that Harvey made a very different sort of friend.

When Marcus had taken off with Harvey that morning, Jinia stayed home to get some work done. "I was in the barn with our horses and I got a text message from Marcus that read, 'Harvey is playing with a coyote!'" Jinia recalls. "My heart dropped into my stomach. My first thought was, oh no, that's dangerous! But then he sent a photo and it was clearly friendly—I could hardly believe what I was seeing."

Marcus says that on an earlier walk, he'd seen the coyote on the path, watching them, "but his hair wasn't up, his head wasn't down.

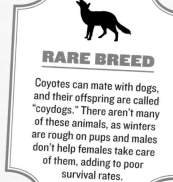

RARE BREED

Coyotes can mate with dogs, and their offspring are called "coydogs." There aren't many of these animals, as winters are rough on pups and males don't help females take care of them, adding to poor survival rates.

He looked curious, not aggressive." Still, Marcus shooed the animal away that time, wary of a bad encounter.

But he kept seeing the coyote, which he started calling Gilbert, and finally, he trusted his gut and let Harvey off leash so the two could truly meet.

Initially, the animals checked each other out warily, and Harvey stayed about 10 feet back from the coyote, running to Marcus if the creature got too close. The meeting was tentative, but the tension was brief. "And then, suddenly, came a burst of happy play," Marcus says. The animals began running around together, chasing, dipping down into play posture with tails in the air, even making gentle contact and splashing at the edge of a lake together. "They played like that for about forty-five minutes, as any two young pups might. It was adorable."

After that, Marcus and Harvey returned to the same area, looking for the coyote, who sometimes sat waiting for them along the hiking path. Once it even followed them all the way back to where they'd parked, and watched them drive away.

When Marcus later posted a video online of the dog and coyote at play, some viewers scolded him for being so reckless with a wild animal, or expressed their disdain for coyotes in general. But

Marcus felt his intuition was good, that the coyote was young, well fed, and not looking for a meal. It was just looking for a friend. "We'd never seen other coyotes around, so this one might have just been lonely," he says. "I didn't sense any ill will or aggression."

Later, Marcus talked to a wildlife expert, who, while stressing that it's best to give wild animals a wide berth, agreed that the situation seemed safe enough. If the coyote were six months older, he told Marcus, it would have been a different story. But an adolescent coyote is still focused on the fun and games that help it to develop life skills. In this case, it found a most unexpected playmate to help it on its way.

Though tentative at first, the pair quickly became playmates.

The
Giving Golden Retriever

DOGS MAKE TERRIFIC BEST FRIENDS. BUT THEY CAN BE so much more. For one boy whose mind rages like a storm, a pup became his shelter, a place to rest his weary head.

Donnie and Harvey Winokur met in their forties. Neither had children but both wanted them, and they found adoption appealing. With family ties to Eastern Europe, they chose to adopt from Russia.

"We applied for two kids, definitely wanting a girl and a boy," Donnie says. The orphans matched with them were one year old when the Winokurs received a photo, a short video, and minimal medical history (nothing notable) on each baby. After a Herculean effort on Donnie's part to speed up the adoption process, the

Winokurs traveled to Russia in 1999 and brought Morasha and Iyal to their home in Atlanta, Georgia.

"Those first weeks were ecstatic, exhilarating, and exhausting at the same time," Donnie says. Initially, both kids seemed to be doing okay. "It wasn't until they were about three that we started to see symptoms in Iyal that made me uncomfortable." Iyal was often hyperactive, or spaced out, and he struggled with simple language. He'd sometimes wake up in a rage.

Many doctors assessed Iyal, and finally there was an answer. The boy had fetal alcohol syndrome (FAS). Because alcohol causes cells to die, his birth mother's drinking had interfered with his brain development. That plus Iyal's year in an orphanage, where he didn't get the attention an infant needs, led to an inability to cope with emotion, among other problems. He had no way to regulate his feelings except by acting out.

So he had tantrums. "But these weren't just a little kid kicking and refusing to do something," Donnie recalls. "They were big. Larger than life. And they kept getting scarier." Therapy wasn't helping Iyal; he was often out of control. "We'd reached a place where everyone was always yelling—at him, at each other," she says. "It was hard on all of us. We were desperate."

And then, Donnie read an article about how service dogs were being trained to help autistic kids and mentally unstable adults, and what she learned gave her hope. Donnie wasn't raised with dogs. "I'd always been a cat person," she says. "But I thought this could be the ticket."

Donnie connected with 4 Paws for Ability, a nonprofit founded by a disabled woman who got her own life on track with the help and love of a service dog. The 4 Paws team chose a golden retriever named Chancer to be Iyal's helper animal. When the young pup reached a certain advanced point in his training, the Winokurs brought him home.

"We knew there were no guarantees, that kids with these kinds of social disorders have trouble bonding," Donnie says. Service dogs are trained to be persistent, but an animal working with Iyal would have to have a deep well of confidence to tolerate the boy's moods. Iyal wasn't always nice and might yell or push a dog away. "We were worried Chancer would have his feelings hurt!" Donnie recalls.

But Chancer turned out to be the right choice. Iyal took to him immediately. He slept with the dog in the crate the first night. "After that, as soon as we'd let Chancer out in the morning, he'd jump up on Iyal's bed and kiss

MIDDAY NAPPERS

Golden retrievers are most active at dawn and dusk, which means they are crepuscular. These dogs were likely bred to be this way, as the early morning light is ideal for hunting (their original job).

him," says Donnie. "Iyal doesn't always like to be touched, but he didn't mind the dog."

Chancer's main job was to sense when Iyal was nearing a meltdown and to help calm him. And he did it well, right from the beginning. "He could sense my son's moods even from another floor of the house," Donnie recalls. "Iyal's grumbling may not even be audible to us, but Chancer would get up and go find him and hang out with him. Sometimes that's all Iyal needs."

And if the boy still lost control, his mother says, "Chancer was there to anchor him. Once his rage dissipated, he would cry and apologize, then tell Chancer, 'I need a nuzzle, I need a hug.' He was asking for his own medication, in a way."

Iyal's hyperactivity is better managed these days. "Unlike kids with ADHD, Iyal doesn't learn from his mistakes. That gap between thought and action doesn't exist," Donnie explains. But with Chancer, the boy's parents have a way to give Iyal something to focus on. "We can say, 'go hang out with Chancer instead

of flying around the house.' And he will just lie there with the dog instead of going crazy when he doesn't know what to do with himself."

But most remarkable have been the more subtle changes, which began appearing early on. "After just two months with

Chancer, at age nine, Iyal started express-ing himself, talking about things he didn't before," says Donnie. "We'd told him he had a boo boo on his brain because his mother drank alcohol while he was devel-oping. Now he'd look at Chancer and ask me, did Chancer's mother drink alcohol? Does Chancer have FAS? This kind of abstract thinking is huge."

Such improvements continue. The dog also gives Iyal a sense of control, and a sense of importance. "Iyal knows Chancer is his dog—he doesn't kiss anyone but Iyal—and he is Chancer's boy. Chancer is there just for him and will respond to his commands." Plus, says Donnie with a laugh, "Chancer is a chick magnet! So now Iyal wants to hold his leash in public. He's no longer embarrassed that people might think he's disabled because of the dog: He loves to share his story."

What does Iyal, now in his late teens, say about Chancer? "I was always upset before I had him. I felt like I didn't have anyone to be with me or help me," he says. "With him, I have someone who is a friend and can help me and who I can love. He makes me feel better and doesn't scold me. And he misses me when I'm gone."

"He's made a really big difference for our family," Iyal says. "He makes it easier for all of us. Especially for me. He understands me better than anyone else."

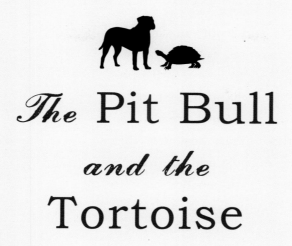

The Pit Bull and the Tortoise

IT'S A SUNNY AFTERNOON IN A BACKYARD IN AZLE, TEXAS, and, as usual, Dolly the pit bull is in a lively mood. She zips around at top speed, kicking up sand and grass, then stops suddenly in front of her best friend and drops down on her elbows, rump up. In canine lingo, it means, "Playtime!"

Dolly's owner, Cynthia Jones, smiles as she watches from her back door. Dolly's play behavior is, in itself, a joy to see. But what makes the romp special is the creature that stands, a bit dazed, in the yard's center. Sheldon is a tortoise, an animal that's not exactly known for its fun-loving nature. So one that plays nicely with a dog, for hours each day, is a rarity among reptiles.

Cynthia, a veterinarian for nearly thirty years, works with

the Humane Society of North Texas on animal cruelty cases, helping to rescue, tend to, and testify in court on behalf of mistreated creatures. Dolly had been taken from a dog-fighting operation. "She was a breeder, not a fighter—at age two, she'd already been pregnant three times and was thin and parasite-infested and depressed," Cynthia says. "I nursed her back to health, and of course got very attached to her. So I brought her home to be a companion for my older lab."

A year later, a call came in from another Texas shelter. They had rescued a tortoise and it desperately needed a place to live. "They didn't know what to do with it, and I have a very good yard for that sort of animal— quite varied, with rocks and cactus plus some grass, sand, mulch, and a grove of trees," Cynthia says. "So I took him home, too."

At first, dog and tortoise were cautious. Sheldon—at 50 pounds, just half grown—hid, as any tortoise would,

pulling his head and legs into his shell, when Dolly approached. They stayed several feet apart while eyeing each other. (Cynthia's other dog simply ignored the new arrival.) But after they circled for a while, their fears dissolved. "Then, they started playing like crazy," Cynthia says. And that's what they've been doing ever since.

Never mind the pit bull's reputation for aggression. Like many of her breed, Dolly is as sweet as she can be. "After having so many litters, she has a great mothering instinct, and it shows," says Cynthia. But her gentle nature doesn't translate to cuddling and sleeping with her friend. Tortoises aren't typically lovey-dovey sorts. The relationship has always been more about fun and games, and sharing—or, in some cases, stealing—resources (as in, food!). Dolly has been known to sneak up and grab a carrot meant for the tortoise. And "the doghouse is now the tortoise house," says Cynthia. "Sheldon has taken it over."

If Sheldon could talk, he'd probably grumble and complain (think Eeyore of *Winnie-the-Pooh*). The tortoise's routine is rock solid: He grazes through the day, shuffles to bed early (in the doghouse-turned-tortoise-house), and sleeps as late as he pleases. Despite his protective shell, too much sun bothers him, as does rain; storms make him grumpy and send him back to bed. And beware of bathtime: One spray from the hose and he'll hiss and turn his back in annoyance. He's . . . reptilian. Moody.

But when he's all napped out and feeling frisky on a dry, mild day, Sheldon happily cavorts with his mammalian friend. And if

Dolly is trying to sleep, Sheldon can be quite a pest—bumping or even nipping the dog to get her attention.

Then the games begin. Dolly romps, running after Sheldon, skidding to a stop just before crashing, then zipping the other way. Sheldon follows suit—turning and running (yes, running!) behind Dolly until Dolly stops, drops, and barks in return. They don't play with toys, although Dolly has tried to interest Sheldon in a red ball. Apparently, reptiles don't "fetch." Still, for a tortoise, Sheldon is oddly puppy-like. And that makes Dolly a very happy pup herself.

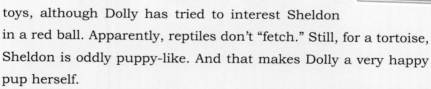

CREEPING ALONG

A tortoise is a turtle, but a turtle isn't a tortoise. A turtle is any shelled reptile of the order Chelonii. The term *tortoise* is more specific, referring to terrestrial turtles (with an exception or two). A group of tortoises is called a "creep," although the animals are usually solitary.

Most of us have spent time around dogs, but tortoises are less familiar. Sheldon is a sulcata tortoise, also called an African spurred tortoise. The species is native to the Sahel and the Sahara Desert of North Africa. Picky about climate, these animals dig deep burrows (sometimes ten feet down) and hide there during the heat of the day.

Another cool fact: The sulcata is one of the biggest tortoise species on Earth, becoming a boulder of an adult, at more than 100 pounds. They can also live for 100 years! "That's something to consider if you are thinking of getting a pet tortoise," Cynthia says. "I've already told my son that he's going to end up caring for this one."

Guess her son will also need a series of dogs, perhaps playful pit bulls, to keep old Sheldon company for the next half-century.

The Fox *and* the Hound

TRUTH SOMETIMES MIRRORS FICTION, AND IN THIS CASE the real thing comes awfully close to the animated story. Disney's version of *The Fox and the Hound* was plenty sweet: Though instinct and social pressure to be adversaries pull childhood friends apart, their loving bond is never truly broken. Now meet Copper and Jack, the living, breathing fairy tale.

Copper is a male fox who, like many animals in these stories, got off to a rough start. He was an orphan—on his own in a grassy field for at least a few days after birth. And then, somehow he managed to fall into a rocky pit in the back garden of a rural home. Luckily, a tangle of ivy caught him as he fell, preventing what might have been a deadly landing. Fortune shined on him again when his squealing cries met the garden owners' ears. Not knowing how to handle the little animal, they called on animal expert Gary Zammit to come rescue him.

Gary runs the Feadon Farm Wildlife Center in Cornwall, England, an 80-acre patchwork of grasslands, woodlands, and ponds. Visitors come to get up close to the wild roe deer, badgers, reindeer, hedgehogs, owls, hawks, and, of course, foxes.

"When I rescued Copper, he was probably a week or two old," Gary says. "But he still needed bottle-feeding 'round the clock. He was dehydrated and in poor condition—hadn't had food for days. We don't know what happened to Mom or the rest of the litter, and this guy wouldn't have survived much longer on his own."

Copper was quite vocal, which stirred the interest of another animal at the center, Jack the dog.

Jack is a lurcher, a hound mix whose breed originated in Ireland and England. Like Copper, he had a sad beginning—his at the hands of an unfeeling owner. Soon after birth, the owner scooped up the entire litter and took them to the vet to be put to sleep because she thought they were ugly! Of course, the vet refused to kill the pups and instead found homes for them.

"I hadn't planned to have another dog, but after getting to know Jack, we had to have him," Gary says. "He's so lovely and affectionate, walks around among the chickens, goats, and ducks without chasing them. He has no hunting instinct at all. A wonderful animal."

But Jack had never really mixed with foxes before (there

were two others at the facility when Copper came). Even though he wasn't an aggressive sort, Gary says, "most dogs would attack and kill a fox, so we never thought to put them together. Copper at that point would have fit nicely into Jack's mouth, so we had to be cautious." But Jack kept coming around to see what the fuss was about. His interest was piqued by the squealing cub and he wasn't going to back down. Gary finally decided to let the dog inspect the new arrival.

"There were no signs of aggression, just a wagging tail and other friendly gestures," he says. "The fox cub, meanwhile, latched on to Jack right away. He was submissive, rolling over to show his belly, squealing and squeaking. After that, he wanted to be with Jack all the time." So fox and hound became napping buddies, spooning for hours at a time, with plenty of reciprocal muzzle licking. And they love to play together: The two charge around the house and wrestle until fully exhausted, and somehow Jack knows to be gentle. If things get a little rough, a tiny yelp from Copper settles the dog right down. Jack wears a bell around his neck, and Gary says Copper quickly associated the sound with his new friend. "When he hears it, he wags his tail and calls, searching around for the dog, wanting to play. They're totally devoted to each other, even though Copper now has other foxes in his life."

This time, truth is even sweeter than fiction.

RED FOX

That beautiful fluffy tail (hidden, below) performs many tasks: It gives the fox better balance, serves as a warm blanket on cold nights, and is used like a signal flag in fox-to-fox communication.

The
Unexpected
Lifeguard

IMAGINE YOU ARE ON A **C**ALIFORNIA BEACH LATE ONE afternoon, dragging a boogie board along the sand behind you. It's windy, not as warm and sunny as you'd hoped. The water looks a bit choppy and it's pretty darn cold. But you've never been to California before, nor swum in the Pacific Ocean, and you're leaving town tomorrow. This is your only chance to have the full California surf experience. So, you wade into the water, flop onto your board, and start paddling out to sea.

Perhaps this was how a couple got in over their heads one summer day, trying to ride a few Pacific waves. They might have met a tragic end had it not been for the quick actions of a four-legged, furry-backed rescuer.

Daniel Clarke was a beach regular, running with Nico, a stunning Bernese mountain dog he and his wife had adopted just a few months before. The day they learned he was theirs, they'd brought him to the beach and let him off leash. Nico was ecstatic, racing along the warm sand, loving the sea spray, and he leaped and played at the water's edge as if he'd never been so free before. "But he wasn't really a swimmer," Daniel says. On that day and on subsequent beach visits, "he never went far beyond the shallow surf."

Then came that windy afternoon. Daniel and Nico were kicking up sand a ways up the beach when Daniel spotted a woman on a boogie board about 50 yards out. "She was in the rip," Daniel says, meaning a rip current, which is a very strong, narrow current that moves directly away from shore, cutting through the breaking waves. Rip currents can easily suck even a strong swimmer out into deeper water; they're the reason for most lifeguard rescues. (The trick to escaping a rip current is to swim parallel to the shore, rather than toward it, until you're free of the current's grip; then head to land.)

Daniel could see the woman was in trouble, and that she was starting to get off her board—which was a bad idea. "I was a lifeguard for years, and you never let go of your lifesaving device," he says. Then he spotted her husband and realized he was making the same mistake, abandoning his board to go after his wife. "At this point I was yelling to them, telling them to get back on their boards, not to panic, that I was going to come get them. I kicked off my shoes and tossed my phone down and started wading in."

And then, suddenly, Nico flew past him, charging into the water straight toward the couple. "And I'm thinking, *Oh no, now the dog is in the rip, too!*" says Daniel. But instead of getting caught, Nico powered through and circled behind the man. For a moment Daniel worried that the people might try to climb on the dog and drown him in their panic. But then, he had an idea. "I yelled, 'Grab his tail!' He has the biggest tail I've ever seen on a dog, it knocks things over all the time. So the guy grabs it and pulls, and *boom*, Nico stops, looks at me, then just keeps powering all the way to shore, huffing and puffing, with the guy holding on."

And once the man was safe, Nico turned, did a classic big-dog shake-off, and headed back into the surf. "Again, he stopped for a moment to look at me, like he was asking my permission," his owner says. "To prompt him, I pretended to throw something in the swimmer's direction. He fought his way back out, circled around the

woman, and let her grab on to the thick coat behind his neck. He pulled her all the way in, too."

As the rescued couple lay on the sand catching their breath, Daniel says, they all just looked at one another and at the dog as if they couldn't believe what had occurred. "We kept saying to each other, 'Did that really just happen?' And the woman asked if Nico had special training, which he doesn't. She thought that was incredible."

But Nico wasn't quite finished demonstrating his superpowers. Once word got out about the dog's heroics, and a news crew came to interview Daniel (and Nico) at the beach, "The dog did it again!" Daniel says. "There was a woman swimming next to the rip, kind of on the edge of it, and Nico just took off after her. The news crew shot it all: Nico walked in by her side, as if making sure she was okay, with the cameras rolling. Then he ran back to me and sat there like it was no big deal.

PULLING THEIR WEIGHT

Big, fluffy Bernese mountain dogs worked for generations in the Bernese Oberland of Switzerland, hauling dairy products—milk, cream, cheese—in wheeled carts, from farms to the dairy. Often children accompanied them on their runs, but the dogs also did just fine on their own.

I'm thinking, *Wow, now he's saved a third person!*" (If Nico was looking for fame, he got it: The video of the save has been a massive hit on YouTube.)

Daniel thinks Nico has changed a tiny bit since his good deeds, that he has a little extra swagger in his step, as he should. "We had no idea he could do something like this, even though we knew he's really loyal and protective. I keep wondering what was going on in his head. He seemed not to think, but just do, and I was grateful because I wasn't looking forward to fighting the rip myself in that wind and fifty-five-degree water."

"He's a real people dog," adds Daniel, "and he certainly proved it that day."

The grateful swimmer is now one of Nico's biggest fans.

The Belgian Malinois *and the* Pygmy Owl

"**I**NGO ISN'T A LOVING DOG. HE'S NOT ALWAYS EVEN A nice dog." That's what Tanja Brandt says about her Malinois—hardly what you'd expect an owner to say of her beloved pet. But this animal is no lick-your-face lab; he's temperamental, "especially toward other dogs or cats." He likes action, Tanja says, so he'll play with people. But he doesn't seek their affection, and mostly he just ignores other animals entirely.

There's one exception (well, two, if you count Tanja). Ingo likes Poldi. A lot. The pygmy owl seems to bring out the best in him, a generous and gentle side. "We go on walks and Ingo runs alongside me as Poldi takes to the air," Tanja says. "They'll rest together on a bench and watch deer. And they tease each other all the time,

like when Poldi nibbles Ingo's ear."

An owl and a dog would normally occupy very separate worlds. But these two have found common ground in their quiet friendship.

Ingo was eight weeks old when he came from a breeder in the Czech Republic to live with Tanja in Düsseldorf, Germany. Having worked with and loved birds of prey, she later brought home Poldi, who was five months old at the time. For all his moodiness around other animals, Ingo seems okay with raptors in general. He shows neither fear nor aggression toward any of Tanja's birds, even though one of her Harris's hawks complains loudly when he's around. "Ingo tries [to get along], but she isn't interested in him. Still, he is always nice to all the birds."

Tanja's other three dogs have not won the raptors over. "The birds don't like them, not at all. They scream and shriek when they see them coming around." Only when Ingo visits do Poldi and

Phoenix (the friendlier hawk) "let out happy sounds," she says. "They seem relieved that it's him." And it's him much of the time: Ingo visits the birds as often as he's invited (and even when he's not). Any time Tanja goes outside to the aviary, "he always has to tag along. Otherwise, he makes a racket with his howling." It's during these daily rounds that Ingo's emotions really break through his stony exterior. When he hears Poldi's high-pitched *toot* and sees the bird looking down at him, Tanja says, "He is gleeful. He and the owl have a really special connection."

Meanwhile, Poldi can't be left alone with the hawks, for good reason, Tanja says. "They'd eat him." In fact, once one of the hawks attacked the owl. "She injured his foot, so I brought him inside and left him on the bed with Ingo while I went to get disinfectant," recalls Tanja. "When I came back, Ingo was very carefully licking Poldi's hurt foot. He watched over his little friend that night." The two even ended up under the covers together.

As is often the case with animals, "the little one is the boss!" Tanja says Poldi has always been in charge of the relationship: "When he is in a bad mood, for example, Ingo is sensitive to that and becomes very small" to stay out of the bird's way. "He knows Poldi wants to have the last word."

And the dog (who no doubt could take control) gives it to him.

When the mood is good, the two are easy friends and couldn't be a better pair of models for a photographer like Tanja. One moment they're a stunning couple, posing tranquilly in a wildflower meadow or by a bubbling stream. The next moment they're cozying up like sweethearts, revealing that unique closeness and trust. And finally, on break from their usual poise, they'll goof off: The owl perches on the dog's head, the two share a silly stuffed toy, or the pair hides together under a blanket. Beauty, friendship, silliness—it's a perfect blend that, all together, makes joy.

Which is what Tanja feels around her unique assortment of pets. "The animals are my happiness," she says. When she's photographing them together, and especially when Ingo is unleashed and running alongside her with Poldi or the hawks flying above them, "they all stay with me and it's so lovely. Ingo, the birds, and I, we're a team."

DOING THE TWIST

It's a myth that owls can rotate their heads 360 degrees. In truth, the birds can turn their necks 135 degrees in either direction, which gives them 270 degrees of total movement. Bone and vascular adaptations allow for this swiveling to occur without cutting off blood to the brain.

The Elephant
and the
Stray Dog

AT THE ELEPHANT SANCTUARY IN HOHENWALD, TENNESSEE, elephants brought together from different parts of the world tend to find a friend among the masses—not surprising for social animals used to life in a herd. Stray dogs, common on sanctuary property, typically ignore the elephants, remaining solo or pairing off with their own kind. Then came an elephant named Tarra and a dog named Bella to break the mold.

Stepping over social traditions, these two intelligent mammals found each other, then rarely parted. The gentle giant and the chubby mutt ate, drank, and slept in tandem. Tarra's tree-trunk legs towered over her canine friend's head, but the two were content as long as they were side by side. Then Bella the dog grew ill, and the staff of the sanctuary took her inside to care for her. Tarra seemed distressed and stayed near the house where Bella lay as if holding vigil for her. For many days, as Bella slowly recovered, Tarra waited. Finally, the two were reunited. Tarra caressed Bella with her trunk and trumpeted, stamping her feet. Bella, all dog, wiggled her whole body in excitement, tongue and tail in a nonstop wag as she rolled on the ground.

And, in a most remarkable moment, Tarra lifted one immense foot into the air and carefully rubbed the belly of her friend.

Renowned biologist Joyce Poole, who may have logged more hours watching elephants be elephants than anyone on Earth, recalls meeting the pair on a visit to the facility: "I was fortunate to get up close and personal, to see Tarra with both Bella and another dog she'd befriended. She kept trying to cradle the dogs with her trunk. It was delightful to see."

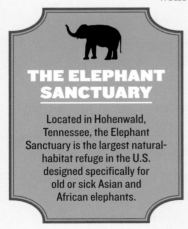

THE ELEPHANT SANCTUARY

Located in Hohenwald, Tennessee, the Elephant Sanctuary is the largest natural-habitat refuge in the U.S. designed specifically for old or sick Asian and African elephants.

But to Poole, such a friendship isn't all that surprising. "We know from our work with elephants, and from our own relationships with dogs, that both animals are very emotional and form close bonds," she says. In the wild, elephants are loyal to tight-knit groups under the influence of a matriarch. They not only adopt one another's young, but they even mourn their dead. An elephant like Tarra, Poole says, who grew up with a mix of role models and was exposed to other species, "has simply shifted that attachment to another kind of animal."

Like Dr. Seuss's famously committed cartoon elephant Horton, who sat in for a wayward mother bird to hatch her egg, it appears that Tarra was "faithful, 100 percent!"

A truly giant friendship.

Two Stories *of* Lifesaving Loyalty

TILLIE AND PHOEBE

FOR A DOG OWNER, WHAT'S SCARIER THAN YOUR BELOVED pet going missing? Two pets missing! So for B.J. Duft, who lives on Vashon Island near Seattle, it was a doubly bad day when his two pups escaped from the yard and didn't come home for dinner.

Phoebe, a young basset hound, was a notorious explorer. Tillie, an eleven-year-old Irish setter-retriever mix, was always game to follow Phoebe's lead. So one late-summer day, when the explorer saw an opportunity—a gate ajar—to seek adventure, the pair trotted off down the road, Phoebe's nose to the ground, Tillie's nose at Phoebe's behind.

Even on a smallish island, a determined dog (read: basset hound) can do an impressive disappearing act. So B.J. reached out for help from a nonprofit called Vashon Island Pet Protectors (VIPP), a shelter and rescue organization with a long list of successful pet recoveries. Volunteer Amy Carey immediately coordinated outreach and a search plan; she also posted a notice on Facebook about the lost pets.

On the first day of the search, VIPP received one call from someone who had seen the dogs the night they disappeared. But on the second day, the phones were quiet.

"Based on my experience, I got this little feeling in my belly," says Amy, "that the dogs were stuck."

It wouldn't be the first time. "We've had dogs stuck in chicken coops, in sheds and barns, in wells," Amy says. The team continued searching in earnest, "but it's like finding a needle in a haystack. I worried that they were somewhere without water or, worse yet, *in* water. That can have a very sad ending."

Owner B.J. was distraught, Amy recalls. He said he tried to keep in mind that there aren't big predators on the island, plus the dogs had

B.J. and his pups at the Washington Capitol, where Tillie received an award from the governor.

wandered before without incident. But his pets had never been gone so long. Also, "Phoebe could easily get back on her own, but Tillie, who is older, gets tired and could get left behind."

The search continued for a week with no leads. And then a hopeful call came: A man about two miles from B.J.'s home had spotted an old red dog several times. "She wouldn't come all the way up to the man, but she'd stand near him, then turn and disappear into a nearby ravine," says Amy. It seemed the dog was asking the man to follow.

ON THE DOWN LOW

The droopy eyed, low-to-the-ground basset hound resulted from selective breeding by French monks in the 1500s. They wanted an animal that could easily follow the scent of small game, so they deliberately bred for short legs and a powerful nose.

Amy went to check the area. At the bottom of the ravine, "I briefly called out, 'Tillie!' though I didn't expect an answer. Missing dogs that are scared or stuck rarely respond vocally."

But then came the surprise: "I got a single *woof* in reply! That gave me a direction point, so I started heading down a deer trail and through some brambles. My skin was tingling and I thought, *Holy wow! They're here!*"

As Amy came around a tangle of blackberry bushes, there was Tillie. "She was pressed as tight as she could be to the lip of a cistern coming up out of the ground," she recalls, "with her head resting on top of the concrete wall, looking down into it. She wouldn't move, wouldn't come to me." She was intent on pointing with her nose to something inside.

Amy's heart pounded, alternating beats of excitement and dread. At first, "I couldn't see inside the cistern, but I thought,

Happy to be home.

Phoebe is in there. Is she dead or alive?"

Happily, Phoebe was alive and well. The cistern wasn't deep, but basset hounds have short legs and limited leaping power, and there was water inside. Fortunately, Phoebe had found a perch atop a pile of rubble and had stayed relatively dry.

"As soon as I saw her, I said 'Phoebe!' and Tillie's whole demeanor shifted," Amy says. "She went from alert mode to a happy, tail-wagging stance. She clearly understood that I was there to help her friend."

Amy immediately called B.J. "I had such a lump in my throat," she says. She was especially moved by Tillie's long vigil that must have helped keep Phoebe calm for so long.

When B.J. arrived, "both dogs suddenly exploded with joy," Amy recalls. "Phoebe was trying to launch herself up and out, and Tillie was wiggling around happily."

As B.J. approached, Tillie barked excitedly but still wouldn't move from her post. She seemed unable to relax until Phoebe was safe. B.J. got in, scooped Phoebe up, and, once all six legs were back on dry land, the happy reunion began. He knelt down and the two dogs danced around him. "There were lots of licks and kisses," he recalls.

Despite Tillie and Phoebe's ordeal, when they got home, both dogs scarfed down a hearty dinner and went back to wrestling and playing ball. And very shortly, "Phoebe was sniffing over by the fence looking for a way out," their owner says, laughing. "She's dominated by that nose. She's an explorer at heart."

Amy posted an update on Facebook, this time with a joyful message: *Missing dogs found! Hooray for Tillie . . . and a Huge Hankie Alert!* Online friends marveled that the old dog had spent so many days watching over her trapped friend.

"It was very humbling to witness that quiet but firm loyalty between two animals," Amy says. When she thinks about it now, "It takes my breath away."

RAZOR AND JAZZY

PUT A SAINT BERNARD and a dachshund in a sticky situation, and it seems logical that the bigger dog would step up and save the day. Saint Bernards are, after all, powerful animals originally bred to rescue travelers caught in alpine snows.

But let's not allow our expectations to get ahead of

us. This story proves that a hero may not look the part. In this case, the dog that stepped up did so from very low to the ground.

It started as a typical Sunday morning, with Tim Chavez of Belen, New Mexico, cleaning up around the yard. "I was in and out, back and forth, and I was a little lax about the gate—I wasn't latching it every time," he says. Tim's dogs were out with him and seemed content lounging in the sun, but when a strong wind gust flung the gate wide open, they took off.

It's likely that Razor, the dachshund, initiated the great escape: "He's the typical little dog among bigger dogs," Tim says, "always acting like he's in charge. Jazzy [the Saint Bernard] looks more intimidating, but she's just sweet and affectionate, always wanting to be petted." Again, looks can be deceptive!

Tim wasn't worried at first. Out in the boonies where he lives, dogs get loose from time to time, roam around for a bit, then go home. "I figured they'd stretch their legs and then come back for dinner," he says. But as the sun started to go down, Tim decided to check the neighborhood. "I hopped in my truck and drove around for a while looking, but no dogs."

FEARLESS HUNTERS

Don't be fooled by its size: The dachshund is no wimp! Germans originally bred the little dog to hunt badgers— tenacious animals with nasty tempers reputed to attack even tractors that come too close to their dens.

When he returned, he was happy to learn that Razor was back in the yard. But there was still no sign of Jazzy. Again, Tim told himself, the dog would come home soon. "I figured I'd wake up in the morning and she'd be there by the water bucket," he says.

But when morning came, Jazzy wasn't there. And Razor was running back and forth, acting frantic. "Normally, he'll focus on his food, but not that day," Tim recalls. "He was trying to get my attention. In hindsight,

it's easy to see, but I didn't realize it then." Tim took one more ride around the area looking for Jazzy, but then he had to go to work. He posted a note on social media, asked a neighbor to lock the dog in if she returned, then rang the police to alert them—in case anyone called in a sighting of a big, scary dog on the loose. ("I was sure to tell them this was a gentle, kind animal," he says.)

A couple of hours later, Tim got a call from his nephew. The young man happened to be at the vet, with his sick cat, when he heard someone from animal rescue saying, "We need help! We have a huge dog that was just rescued from an irrigation ditch!" He ran out to help unload the animal and realized, *Hey, that's my uncle's dog!*

Jazzy was a mess, and hypothermic, but her mud-caked tail went mad wagging when she saw Tim come into the clinic. It was a happy—if very soggy—reunion. The dog had been in a ditch, in more than three feet of water and mud, for as many as eighteen hours. "She has arthritis and hip dysplasia, and probably exerted all her strength when she first got stuck," Tim says. "Then she just hung on, keeping her nose in the air, trying to stay alive."

Tim soon found out that Jazzy was rescued because Razor kept returning to the scene and barking nonstop, trying to get someone's attention. Eventually, passersby followed the upset pup to the edge of the ditch. When they saw Jazzy trapped below, they called for aid.

Razor's effort to help his friend had been going on all day. Before the rescue, while Tim was at work, Razor had been pestering a neighbor, barking and running back and forth just as he had with Tim that morning. The neighbor thought the dog was irritating and shooed him back toward his own yard. But instead of going home, Razor returned to the ditch and continued to sound the alarm until someone finally responded.

As a team from the Belen Fire and Rescue pulled Jazzy to safety that afternoon, Razor was at their heels, darting around, barking, perhaps letting his friend know he was there for her. And these days, says Tim, "They're inseparable. Jazzy will be basking in the sun and Razor will lie across her tail or belly, just staying really close. For a while they even ate out of the same bowl at the same time, which they hadn't before."

Looking back, Tim says, "I'm sure that's why Razor was so frantic that morning. How did I not catch on that he knew something? It makes me sad that I didn't know, that it took so long to get Jazzy out of there. I've got to learn to pay more attention to the

Tim with the big victim and the little hero.

small things, things you might not think are important."

He's kicking himself especially hard because, he says (a little embarrassed), Jazzy had gotten herself stuck in that same ditch some five years before. And oddly, another small dog—a little poodle Tim owned at the time—had done what Razor had, making a lot of noise until someone came to help.

"No one caught that first rescue on camera," Tim says, "so I guess Jazzy felt the need to do it again, for a little fame. So there's something else I learned from this experience. Jazzy loves the spotlight!"

Thanks to two Maremma sheepdogs, Middle Island's little penguin population has grown from seven to 200.

The Keepers of *the* Little Penguins

ON THE SEA-BEATEN COASTS OF SOUTHERN AUSTRALIA and New Zealand lives the smallest penguin on Earth. It is appropriately called the little penguin (or, delightfully, the fairy penguin), and it is a gem of a bird, tidily dressed in a hooded cape of blue, with a white belly and hazel eyes. A breeding colony of these unique birds lives on Middle Island, a chunk of rock off Victoria, Australia, near the city of Warrnambool. At sunrise, the penguins go to sea to catch and eat fish, squid, and other small swimmers, and come back onto shore at dark. They usually forage for food in shallow water but sometimes dive as deep as 65 feet. Life is good in their Middle Island habitat, with its food-rich waters and perfect sites for egg-laying burrows.

Eudy and Tula on fox patrol.

Except there's one big problem. During November and December, at low tide, the water becomes so shallow that foxes can slink over from the mainland on a bridge of sand. (They'll even swim over, if they have to, but they prefer to keep their furry selves dry.) Foxes love penguins, but not in the nice way. To them, the little birds are tasty morsels, easily hunted down. At one time, the foxes were so thorough in their harvest that the Middle Island penguin population, which before the year 2000 had been around 600 birds, declined to just 7 animals in 2005.

I should mention that despite the slaughter on Middle Island, little penguins aren't an endangered species; they're not even

considered threatened. Although domestic cats and dogs have taken out many mainland colonies in their native Australia and New Zealand, they are still plentiful on the coasts and islands. There are probably about a million of them throughout their range. But this particular group was clearly in big trouble. And mainland residents are attached to Middle Island's penguins. The birds are a part of the local landscape and culture, so folks wanted to bring the population back.

City Council staff tried everything to pick off the offending foxes, from baiting to fumigating the island to playing sniper. But none was a long-term solution. So in 2006, the council, the Warrnambool Coastcare Landcare Group, and community volunteers decided to unite and enlist a special guarding force. They chose the burly and beautiful Maremma sheepdog to do the job, in an effort called the Middle Island Maremma Project. Sheepdogs are certainly excellent protectors of livestock, and as one chicken farmer put it, "to dogs, penguins are only chooks [slang for chickens] in dinner suits." Still, it was an experiment.

DRAMATIC DEFENSE

In a dramatic move before the dogs came along, the Australian parks service once hired professional snipers to defend the besieged colony of little penguins from fox attacks.

Happily, it worked beautifully. The Maremmas turned out to be perfect penguin protectors. From the beginning, foxes were sent packing and the penguin numbers slowly began to rise. Less than a decade later, the population is estimated to be nearing 200, a big jump from seven. The current heroes to the penguins are a pair of young Maremmas, Eudy and Tula, who live and work on the island from September into April. Eudy is a bit of a loner—happy to check people out but then go about her business. Tula is the social one, the tail wagger, always happy to see you. They've bonded with the land, the volunteers and staff, the birds, and each other. And they take their job very seriously, patroling the island each morning to look for and drive out any intruders, then keeping watch throughout the day and night—snoozing on and off when all is quiet.

"One reason we picked this breed is that they think before they act," explains Paul Hartrick from the Warrnambool City Council. "Ordinary domestic dogs just bark their heads off. But these animals only bark if another dog or a fox gets too close and becomes an actual threat. That's when they act." If a fox is near, the dogs will herd the penguins together and stand between them and the predator, he says. "And if the fox moves in, then they'll chase."

To help this program to thrive, the island has been closed to the public since 2006 and will remain that way for the forseeable future. The community has given this idea its blessing, realizing that for these beloved penguins to keep reproducing successfully,

they need some privacy. Having people scrambling over the rocks and beaches snapping photos could interfere with this essential behavior. Meanwhile, not wanting to lock the public out entirely, the Warrnambool City Council runs tours every summer to give people a glimpse of the little penguins and the Maremmas that protect them.

These dogs probably don't realize they are providing such a heroic service, of course. But says Paul, "They dedicate their lives to protecting these penguins, and they really seem to enjoy their role."

On behalf of the little fairies, a big thanks to their furry protectors!

The Mama Pit Bull *and* Her Precious Kittens

SOME WOMEN ARE MEANT TO BE MOTHERS. **F**ROM EARLY on, they feel a visceral need to cuddle infants, and will pursue motherhood for as long as it takes. Being a parent makes them feel whole.

This story is about a dog that has that same yearning, to protect and dote on a little one in the way that only mothers can do. And what's special about this animal is that she's content to mother babies that aren't her own—that aren't even of the same species. For her, if it's furry, squirmy, hungry, and helpless, she'll give it all the love she has.

This powerfully maternal pup is named Pitty (she's a pit bull) and she was picked up as a stray in Dallas, Texas. Her history

is uncertain, but her rescuers think it might include a junkyard and men treating her poorly. (A year after rescue, she still had a strong fear of men in black clothing.) When she was discovered on the street, her body revealed that she'd recently given birth, but sadly there were no puppies found with her.

That's not to say there was no baby in her care. There was one, in fact. It was a tiny kitten, perhaps five days old with eyes not yet open, and the rescuers found it latched on to one of the dog's nipples, suckling, as if the dog were its natural mother.

"After twenty-nine years in veterinary practice, I still found this unusual!" says Dr. Rick Hamlin of Mercy Animal Hospital, where the pair ended up after they were rescued. The dog was thin and hungry herself, but she allowed the kitten, soon called "Kitty," to feed from her (she was still producing milk from having recently given birth) and would then gently lick her clean. "We kept them in a large cage together during the day," Rick says, "and Kitty was usually attached to

UNFAIR REPUTE

Pit bulls are reputed to be aggressive, but their temperaments vary like any other breed, and most are perfectly sweet. In fact, you are sixty times more likely to be killed by falling coconuts than from a pitbull attack. Watch out for those palm trees!

the dog during that time. I had to take the kitten home at night, and the first time I separated them, Pitty became distressed and howled a mournful cry."

The Mercy staff cared day and night for the unlikely duo, bottle-feeding Kitty to help her gain weight. Pitty's milk had nearly run dry when the two were brought in, "so the fact

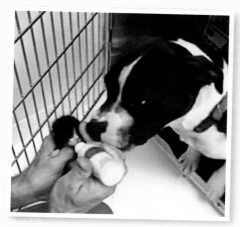

Bottle-fed and Pitty-licked!

that they were found when they were was lifesaving for Kitty," Hamlin says. "Who knows how they came to be together on the side of a rural road, but clearly Pitty's maternal instinct was strong enough to know what to do" for the motherless animal. And her gentle, sweet character meant she did it just right.

Despite the best efforts of Pitty and the doctors, the kitten passed away shortly after the rescue. It turned out she had a congenital malformation, or a birth defect, that became deadly. There was nothing to be done for her, but it was comforting for all involved to know she'd had Pitty's affection in her final days.

Often, if a mother cat or other mammal senses a weakness or illness in one of her young, she may abandon it—in order to preserve her milk and attention for the babies more likely to survive. That may be what happened to Kitty before Pitty took her in. The mama cat might have realized Kitty wouldn't live long and so pushed her away. (It sounds cruel, but it makes sense in the animal world, where resources may be limited.)

Meanwhile, Pitty was healthy and, though still thin and a bit wary of people, she was ready for a new home and family.

Mina Smirnova had heard about the kitten-loving dog on the news and wanted to adopt her. She had three cats and two other dogs already, but plenty more love to give. Quickly, she got in touch with the veterinary clinic and pitched herself to Dr. Hamlin, who agreed she'd be the perfect one to take Pitty home.

From day one, Mina says, Pitty seemed to be a bit lost without the tiny feline to whom she'd given so much. After all, except at night, they'd spent every minute together before Kitty died. "When we first let her into the house, she was running around, sniffing the corners and under the furniture, really crying and upset," says Mina. "We're sure she was looking for Kitty."

She settled down a bit after that, but still, it seemed like something was missing for her. And then, unexpectedly, Pitty got the happy chance to mother another tiny feline.

Mina's boyfriend, a policeman, strolled in one stormy night with a stray kitten that he'd found drenched and mewing in a mud puddle during his shift. It was probably about two weeks old and

Caring for the first Kitty.

Pitty's second chance.

"a bit of a mess," Mina says. She bathed and swaddled the little animal, then gave her over to Pitty—who was clearly anxious to be included.

"They bonded immediately," Mina says. "And for the next two weeks, as we nursed the kitten to health, Pitty babysat her, guarding that kitten literally all the time. She didn't want to be away from her, so she would stand over her, lick her, and cuddle with her. The kitten was a little scared at first of this big dog, but soon she was okay with the attention" and started giving some in return.

The two are truly family now (along with the rest of Mina's menagerie), and Pitty still watches over the baby like a proud but nervous mom. "I have to wonder whether Pitty thinks Kitty II is the same animal she was caring for before," Mina says. But whether the dog knows the difference, "it's a blessing that it worked out this way. We really think she remembered and was sad to have lost the first kitten. Before, she'd whimper a lot and we'd have to comfort her." Now, with the new baby under her watch, "Pitty is much, much better. She acts like she's found her long-lost love."

Once a mother, always a mother: "She's just happy to have a baby again."

Graham and his two special helpers.

The Seeing Eye Dog *Who* Can't See

A LONG TIME AGO, WHEN THE RADIO STARTED TURNING musicians into pop idols, a new sound emerged—starry-eyed teenage girls screaming. It was a very distinctive noise, and it came from fans too excited and too in love to speak. Recently, that sound rose up on the playground of a school in England. But it wasn't for a handsome guy with a crooning voice or an electric guitar. It was for an old, blind dog named Edward.

Edward, a Labrador retriever with a noble face and laid-back attitude, has become quite famous in his part of England. His owners, Graham and Sandra Waspe, always knew he was clever and smart, but they had no idea that he'd become a local celebrity. When they visited that elementary school, for example, all the starstruck kids just wanted to get close to this unique pup, to stroke his fur and take a photo with him.

Why the attention? It's quite a story.

For years, Edward was Graham's Seeing Eye dog. Graham injured his eyes in separate incidents years ago. He lost his right eye completely in a car crash; the left, hurt in a childhood accident, was then weakened further by glaucoma. Graham has only a bit of residual vision, but when Edward came into his life from a British charity called Guide Dogs (short for the Guide Dogs for the Blind Association), the world opened up again.

So it's sadly poetic that, years later, Edward, too, was stricken with glaucoma, and went blind himself. Here's a dog who had loaned his eyes to another for much of his life, only to lose them completely later on—due to the same disease that impaired his master.

GUIDE DOG STATS

Although there are no precise numbers available, a common estimate is that there are some 10,000 guide dog teams (dog plus handler/owner) in the United States, or that around 2 percent of people in this country who are blind or visually impaired work with guide dogs.

"Edward was already very popular before he lost his sight," says Sandra. She and Graham had been longtime speakers for Guide Dogs "and thousands of people, aged two to one hundred two, had met and loved him."

But with the dog's sight loss came an unexpected outpouring of support. Edward's story made the local, then national, then international news, and suddenly, everyone who didn't know Edward already was clamoring to meet him. In his own mellow way, the old dog still relishes the attention he gets on the streets (and at schools; he truly loves those screaming kids, Sandra says).

Edward (left) and new guide dog Opal.

"He's a show-off. He has a funny pose—lying down on one shoulder with his bottom sticking up," she explains. "We call it the shoulder stand. He stays like that until the audience responds with an *awwwwww,* which they always do."

From there, Edward rolls onto his back and waves his legs in the air. "It makes everyone laugh, and it looks like he's smiling, too," says Sandra. It's one of the little behaviors that makes Edward Edward.

Stardom hasn't ruined the blind dog, and to Graham, he has simply been the constant companion who made it possible for the sixty-six-year-old to get on with life despite faulty eyes. "It's really amazing how well guide dogs help us to cope," he says. "Before Edward, I'd walk into posts and trip a lot. But he brought me more than just help with that sort of thing. Our partnership really made my life much better." That love between animal and master is especially powerful, he says, when it's more man relying on dog than the other way around.

But Edward isn't the only star in this story. When the older Lab's eyes failed him, Graham knew he'd have to let a new dog into his life. Enter Opal, a younger, yellower version of her predecessor. "It was hard at first," Graham says. "The trainer asked, 'Are you ready for a new dog?' But how can you be ready for that? It was very difficult for me to go out with Opal and leave Edward behind. He would come to the door and want to come with us. Edward was the one I wanted by my side."

But Opal, a quick study when it came to guide-dog skills (perhaps learning a few of them from wise Edward's behavior), proved her love and worth, and solidified her place in the family. From the day she arrived, Sandra says, Opal has been attached to Graham. "Even after five years, she still follows him from room to room, and watches through the glass door to the garden to get a glimpse of him if they are apart. She was totally his from the start—would pull your arm off to get to him."

Opal (left) sees for all of them.

And now the young Lab sees for both Graham and Edward. Not that Edward needs a lot of help. After so many years as the navigator, he's quite good at making his way around the house and yard without sight. But away from home, Sandra says that she's noticed that Edward will hurry to keep up with Opal, "listening to her feet on the pavement, using her footsteps to help him get along." He also still listens to and follows any commands given to Opal along the way. Though he now plays a different role in the family, "Edward's still part of the pack and wants to be with the rest of us," says Sandra.

Young Opal on a work break.

In his retirement, the older dog often walks with Sandra at the other end of his leash, "usually going somewhere of Edward's choosing," she says.

Meanwhile, Graham takes Opal—or the other way around—out independently. "Edward, and now Opal, have been my mobility, my independence," he says. "I can go to the doctor, to the shops, anywhere and everywhere, because of them. Plus, they're lovely friends. You love them like children."

For the visually impaired, he says, the connection between human and dog "is a unique and intimate bond."

Joker, with some playmates.

The
Salty Dog
and the Dolphins

ON THE SOUTH SIDE OF EILAT IN ISRAEL, WHERE THE
Red Sea creeps onto sandy, tourist-packed shores, a shaggy
dog took a leap of faith.

His name was Joker, and one warm day in the spring of 2000
he simply showed up at Dolphin Reef, a beachy tourist attraction
specializing in encounters with the popular marine mammals. He
belonged to a family in town, but he seemed more at home on the
Reef's wooden pier overlooking the sea.

At first, the owners weren't happy about their canine visi-
tor. They were concerned that he'd chase the cats, chickens, and
peacocks that lived on the property. But Joker kept coming—
traveling every day from wherever he laid his head at night—and

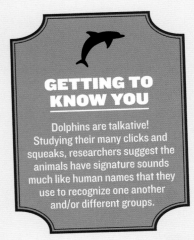

GETTING TO KNOW YOU

Dolphins are talkative! Studying their many clicks and squeaks, researchers suggest the animals have signature sounds much like human names that they use to recognize one another and/or different groups.

never raised a paw to the other animals. In fact, he seemed uninterested in all species but one: the dolphins.

Dolphin Reef has a population of eight bottlenose dolphins all fathered by a male named Cindy, the so-called Don Juan of the pod. (Yes, Cindy is a male.) At times, the animals have been given free access to the open sea and allowed to choose between the Reef and the wild. So while they do encounter humans and receive food, their behaviors remain quite natural—including their play.

Those acrobatics held Joker's interest for many days. He sat on the dock and observed the dolphins as they gathered and squealed and splashed and rocketed through the waves. Then one day during feeding time, Joker abandoned his dry observation post and leaped in.

The dolphins appeared to welcome the dog into their world, so after that first leap his swims became routine. For a time, the Reef staff tied Joker up during feedings to keep him from distracting the dolphins as they ate. Soon the pup realized that he was welcome in the water any time but during a meal. He learned to read the aquatic mammals' signals and "would jump in only when the dolphins were teasing him or inviting him," says Tal Fisher, one of the dolphin trainers.

Joker became a bit of a star, and people who saw him making his daily sojourn from town would pick him up—despite his salty-dog stink—and drop him at his favorite spot. He always headed straight for the wooden pier above the water, where his playful friends would greet him.

Eventually, the dog's owners realized Joker was happiest at the Reef, and they let the mutt move in permanently with the facility owners so he'd have easy access to his aquatic playmates. To this day, he spends many nights sleeping on the dock, ready to start the morning by barking at the dolphins as they congregate below. Then he jumps into the water to frolic with them. "They react by swimming around him and splashing with their tails," says Tal. "They even speak to him."

How dog barks and dolphin squeaks translate across species is a mystery. But the mutually curious animals seem to have discovered a shared language in play.

Swimming partners.

The Harzer Fuchs *and* His Woodland Nursery

HOW BIG IS A DOG'S HEART? WELL, THAT DEPENDS— on the breed, the size of the dog, the shape of the chest. But in Laska's case, physiology really doesn't matter. His heart is the heart of a giant. Even his name means "love" in Czech. It's what he was meant to do.

And he loves freely. He has his own little menagerie on which he dotes. Roe deer. Wild pigs. Raccoon, rabbit, fox, hedgehog. I could go on, but we'd run out of space. As it is, I'll have to narrow it down to three friendships that will squeeze into these pages. (I'm featuring the most reciprocated loves. Hint: Hedgehogs are prickly and not great huggers.)

Laska is a Harzer fuchs, an old German sheepherding breed,

who has lived with his owners, biologists Frank and Katrin Hecker, since he was eight weeks old.

When Katrin got Laska, the seller wasn't sure of his breed. "But the dog grew up looking just like a Harzer fuchs!" And so it was decided. Ever since, he's been the heart of the rather diverse Hecker family in Schleswig-Holstein, northern Germany, helping to raise orphaned animal babies that the Heckers take in. "Laska has shown so many of them the world, teaching them how to cope," says Katrin. "They all follow him everywhere. There is one hundred percent trust between them!"

He is, in a sense, everyone's mother. Well, technically, father. But he's just so motherly that "Mom" seems like the right title.

Among his many relationships, Laska has had three truly special loves, his owners say.

Laska's favorite rough-playing pal.

THE ROE DEER

BACK IN **2009**, TIRZA had lost her mother, and the little fawn was having trouble getting up and running. So she joined the Hecker family, where loving Laska "showed a lot of interest—but we wouldn't dare let him get close because we were afraid he'd frighten her," says Katrin.

But as time passed, Tirza remained stressed and weak. Since human care wasn't working, the Heckers grasped at the possibility that the dog might be a remedy, not a problem. Certain that the gentle pup wouldn't harm the little animal, they introduced dog to deer. "Laska became our last hope."

It was a hope fulfilled. As soon as Laska was allowed near Tirza, he started to sniff her and lick her fur. "The deer calmed down immediately. She obviously loved his smell and touch. And with Laska there, she allowed us to get close and to touch her, too. And finally, to feed her!"

It was a wonderful moment, Katrin says, "when Tirza accepted the milk bottle for the first time, with Laska lying beside her."

And then Laska surprised the Heckers again with his "motherly" instincts. "Small mammals need a stomach rub after each meal, to help them digest. Usually the mother takes care of this gentle tongue massage. Instead, Laska did it—perfectly. And Tirza loved it."

Tirza grew strong and playful under the dog's watch and care, until she was old enough to join other deer in a nearby wildlife park. And eventually, she was released back into the wild. Laska truly had saved her life, loved her well, and let her go—the way a good parent should.

THE LITTLE RACCOON

ONCE UPON A TIME, FRODO THE ORPHAN RACCOON COULD fit in the palm of your hand. But tiny as he was, he made plenty of noise, continually venting his discontent with a squealing vibrato. That's what baby raccoons do, you see, when they're hungry.

"This happened every two hours or less, starting at four thirty in the morning," Katrin says. And the screaming lasted all day. "Quickly we learned it was easiest to just take Frodo and his milk bottle with us wherever we went. So, Frodo was kind of our second dog."

Fortunately, the first pup welcomed this second dog warmly into the family. After every meal, Laska cleaned up Frodo's fur and gave his tummy that little massage with his tongue, much as he did for Tirza the fawn.

Frodo grew up really fast with his canine caretaker's encouragement, becoming Laska's (slightly wilder) shadow. He was fearless and curious and very playful, sometimes hiding from Laska, then jumping out and startling him. Raccoons, as they age, tend to play very roughly. Laska, in his calm and sweet way, was able to tame Frodo a little, teaching him how to hold back those teeth and claws enough to keep from hurting the people (and the dog) who loved him.

And then came the day when Frodo went missing. "We looked everywhere! It was a terrible situation, a lone captive raccoon lost in nature!" Katrin recalls. But Laska wasn't about to give up on his little buddy, and his persistence and good nose paid off. "Suddenly Laska was jumping up against an old tree and barking. We looked up, and there was Frodo. He had discovered he could climb!"

Up turned out to be easier than down. It took some bribing with Laska's treats to get the raccoon to the ground. When they were reunited, Laska ran in circles around his baby, barking but wagging his tail—as if a little upset by Frodo's behavior (as any parent would be) but also quite relieved to have him back safe.

Raccoons, of course, are meant to be with other raccoons. "He became a beautiful and strong adult and soon it was time for him to live his own life, so we had to say goodbye to him,"

SO SENSITIVE

Raccoons have a very advanced sense of touch, in part via whiskers that grow from their fingers. Called *vibrissae*, the little hairlike extensions on their forepaws transfer info about whatever they touch to the brain.

Katrin says. "This was maybe the hardest goodbye for Laska. Dogs and raccoons are alike in many ways and these two really loved and understood each other."

Frodo integrated very quickly into the wildlife preserve and found plenty of his own kind there. And no doubt, he's still there now, roughhousing (maybe a little more gently than some), climbing trees (both up and down), and perhaps remembering those who helped him along the way, especially that generous creature in a soft orange coat—his "mother," his teacher, and his best friend.

THE TWIN BOARS

A PAIR OF WILD BOAR PIGLETS, MOTHERLESS LIKE TIRZA and Frodo, moved from the cold, snowy forest to the Hecker home for some TLC in February 2010. Who gave that special affection to them? Perhaps no longer surprising, it was Laska!

"Both immediately accepted Laska as their 'mother,'" says Katrin, "and anytime Laska lay down, they'd be all over him." Piglets in the wild are feisty and competitive eaters, battling for the best nipple on their mothers. Maybe Alice and Emma, as their owners named them, were looking for milk ducts beneath his fur, Katrin says.

Regardless, "Laska tolerated them with great patience. Believe me, little wild boars require strong nerves!" Laska seemed smitten with them, actually, playing, licking, and nuzzling their wiry little bodies. And the pair followed Laska around, copying his every move, even running with him to the door to greet visitors, doglike, with stubby tails wagging happily.

In the wild, boar piglets stay in their family lair for their first week, then stick close to their mother on her food-finding journeys, learning what's good to eat. (It's a female-dominated society, with mothers and aunts caring for piglets and a big old sow as the leader.) If mom is absent, her babies lie pressed together and wait for her, relying on one another for warmth and comfort.

Of course, Alice and Emma had a warm blanket of a friend in Laska, and they didn't have to wait very long for a meal (which Laska never stole, despite daily temptation). While many boar piglets kept in captivity grow slowly and poorly without their mothers, this is a very different story. With the Heckers in charge and Laska bringing up the rear, these two little piggies—now happy and healthy at a wildlife preserve—have done just fine.

A pair of heroes:
Kona (right) and Kasey.

The Poodles *Who* Loved in *the* Face of Loss

I'VE HEARD A LOT OF STORIES ABOUT SERVICE DOGS, AND each one wiggles into my heart, sits, and stays. But of course I can't include them all here. (Blame my editor, who insists that my books have back covers.) So I've picked a favorite for these pages, a story of loss replaced by love, a tale of good people with broken lives and the heroic dogs who mended them.

It begins with Mike Easter. Mike was a kind, solid man who lived to play drums and dance (though not at the same time), and who loved jazz, sports, and, most of all, family. Life offered Mike some happy times—he played in bands, ran his own auto business, found love (he met his wife, Chris, at nineteen and they were married for fifty years!), and had two great kids.

Mike and young Kona.

But a lot of loss followed. The couple's son died from a heart defect at age five, "and part of Mike died then," says Chris. In the years that followed, type 1 diabetes ravaged his body: He developed neuropathy in his feet, legs, and gut; arthritis snatched the drumsticks from his hands; and near-blindness forced him to give up his business. Blood sugar highs and lows whittled away at his good nature: "He'd turn nasty, banging on tables and yelling—we'd have to run behind him and give him a shot of glucose," Chris recalls. Eventually, he was pretty much housebound in their Maryland home.

This is where the first dog enters the story. Kona is a standard poodle, a tall, dark, and handsome animal who offered Mike an end-of-life friendship like no human could. Because of Kona, Chris says, Mike softened in a way that his family hadn't seen in a long time. Only the birth of their grandkids brought him more joy, she says.

Kona came from Fidos for Freedom, a wonderful organization that trains dogs to help those in need of physical and emotional support. People don't simply show up and trade a wheelchair for the dog they like the most. It's an individualized process that requires a person to work with different dogs and, finally, to train extensively with the animal that suits him or her best. In Mike's case, he and Kona worked together for some eighteen months before he took the pup home.

Kona had received his initial training from prisoners, who had done a fantastic job turning a fun-loving puppy into a rock-solid service animal. The poodle became an extension of Mike; they worked perfectly as a team and were rarely apart. "It was a match made in Heaven," says Chris.

Not only did the dog assist with the basics—retrieving items, opening drawers and doors, acting as Mike's eyes, and helping him keep his balance—"he also gave Mike love and a purpose," says Chris. By the time Kona came to live with them, Mike's eyes were failing and he had very little energy, but having the dog forced him to keep going. He was up daily, feeding, brushing, and walking his companion. He'd sit and throw a ball for Kona, relishing the dog's joy in retrieving it. He also wanted to return the affection that Kona gave freely.

"Their relationship was so special," his wife says. "I'm sure it helped Mike to live longer than he would have otherwise." She recalls Kona going with her to the hospital during one of Mike's stays and standing with his front paws on the bed. "Poor thing couldn't really help Mike then, but just his being there for Mike was everything."

Kona in 2015.

Sadly, Mike passed away from complications of diabetes within a year of

Kona coming home. And while Chris also loved and relied on the poodle, "I always kept in mind why, and for whom, he was there." With Mike gone, Kona no longer had a job to do. Under such circumstances, Fidos for Freedom has a rule: The service dog, rather than becoming a pet for the deceased person's family, gets re-homed with someone else in need.

"Giving up Kona was awful, just awful," says Chris. She had just lost her beloved husband, and now she had to say good-bye to the dog that had meant so much to both of them. "Kona held so many memories for me; he was Mike's shadow that last year, and I couldn't help but think of them together." Of course, she understood the reason for the rule. Kona had so much left to give, but that didn't mean Chris wouldn't mourn the dog's leaving.

Kona's departure left Chris alone with her emotions. The losses had piled up and, finally, they crushed her. Then

Kasey (left) and Kona, together for an afternoon playdate.

GOOD LISTENERS

You may have heard that poodles are among the smartest of all dogs. But did you know they are especially sensitive to vocal intonation? That means they get a lot of information from the tone of your voice—one reason they are easy to train.

Kasey

came a terrific act of kindness. Jim Ballou, the breeder who had donated Kona to Fidos, surprised Chris with the perfect gift: a poodle puppy of her own, named Kasey. Kasey was actually Kona's nephew, a glossy-black, sweet-as-can-be pup who romped into Chris's world and turned her thoughts away from sad things.

He also took every last bit of her energy. "It was a nightmare at first," Chris admits, about having a new puppy in her life. "He was ripping up my yard, jumping on me, eating everything in sight, including furniture cushions and money. The little guy was a lot to take care of."

But Chris kept her eyes on the prize—a dog as loyal and gentle as Kona, perhaps?—and soon pillow-ripping puppyhood was replaced by a smart, generous adulthood. Kasey (his full name is Kasey's Miracle, for the wondrous way he came to her) "filled a big void in my life. And now of course, I can't stand to leave him; I take him with me everywhere I go." He isn't yet a service "hero dog" the way Kona is, but he is already Chris's hero for giving her a purpose, and a lot of love—he's always under hand to get, and give, affection—as Kona did for Mike during his darkest days.

Chris has thought about putting Kasey through the Fidos training program—she's struggling with ill health and pain herself, and could use a service dog's help—and is also considering other jobs for him. "He could be a greeter at a funeral home, or work with grieving families," she says. "Or perhaps he'll be part of a reading program for troubled kids. He's so loving: Whatever he does, it will be something special."

Meanwhile, Kona now lives nearby with a woman named Sandy Ball and, not surprisingly, he's now *her* hero. "I was using a walker and a cane all the time before he came," Sandy says. "With Kona, all that went away." He's quiet and smart, she says, "a statue of a dog that I can trust to stay still, to help me with my balance. He's also a lover and a cuddler, always tucking his head in my lap when I'm sitting and leaning against me while we sleep. He gives me incredible physical and emotional support."

"I was stuck," Sandy admits, "not venturing out to do things by myself; I was scared to live my life. But I'm not scared anymore, because he's always with me. He's changed my life entirely."

Chris says the same thing of Kasey. "The right dog makes all the difference." Can she envision a Kasey-free existence? She shudders a little with an emphatic "no." Still, if Kasey, like Kona, had a job to do and had to move on? Would she take a break from dog ownership and all the work it entails?

"Nope," she says. "I'd have to get another dog quickly. I'd say I'd have one by midweek at the latest."

Sandy with Kona.

Beth and some big kittens.

The Dog *Who* Walked *with* Lions

BETH IS A LION HUNTER. OR, AT LEAST, HALF OF HER is. To clarify, her father was a Rhodesian ridgeback—also called a "lion hound," whose job in the old days in southern Africa was to accompany hunters going after big cats that had killed local livestock. So, genetically speaking, half of her knows lions as quarry.

Beth's mother was a bull mastiff, which is no wimp of a breed, either. Historically, they were nighttime guard dogs for gamekeepers, and they look and act the part. But don't let her breed titles define her. While Beth is an imposing mass of muscle, she's 100 percent old softie, which explains how she came to walk and wrestle with lions with nothing but friendship on her mind.

Beth's original owners were mastiff breeders, and despite her beauty, they considered her an unrefined mutt. She and her littermates were the unplanned result of a fence leap by a ridgeback Romeo looking for a nighttime tryst.

Happily, nearby the breeder's home in Cullinan, South Africa, is the 1,000-acre Horseback Africa reserve, run by Colin and Theony MacRae. Their son Brandon was thrilled to take at least one of the unintended puppies off the breeders' hands.

So Beth grew up on a private game reserve where visitors can do safaris from atop a horse, a safe seat with a great view. What they see is a landscape populated by the kinds of animals that don't sit on your lap while you watch TV. We're talking big stuff— like zebras and giraffes and warthogs. Oh my.

The MacRaes also love lions, and have raised a number of these endangered cats to be released into wildlife reserves or into the African bush. So far, the family has sent cats to Angola and Zambia. It's not trivial work, as lion populations have declined drastically in recent decades—from perhaps 250,000 twenty years ago, to fewer than 20,000 left in the wild now.

MEASURING UP

Lions loom large, but they are actually the second biggest of the big cats. Tigers are number one!

Fewer individuals means lower genetic diversity, which can make the animals less hearty in the face of disease or disaster. Colin says the genetic diversity among lions at Horseback Africa is as high as that of Kruger National Park in South Africa. "So, even though our project is small, we believe it makes a difference," he says.

Meanwhile, the MacRaes' lions attract tourists from all over who want to hop on a horse and walk next to the mightiest cats on Earth.

For many years, Beth joined every tour that included the lions. "That's what Beth loved most—to run right along with us," says Colin. And in a way, he says, Beth and the lions are very similar. "Most big cats

are solitary, but lions are very sociable, the only big cats that live in a pride [the term for a group of lions]. And that side of the lions, that social side, looks a lot like what dogs do."

So, a dog that runs with lions? It seems almost natural (emphasis on *almost*).

Back when Beth was young, she was always game to play with the lion cubs, running, chasing, rolling around, though she maintained her dominance over them. "That's critical," says Colin. "The cats get quite big by a year old, and that could be a bit dangerous for a dog. She had to be above them."

She seemed to know it. Beth wasn't one to let a silly cat, even one that would soon be a formidable predator, get the better of her. "If a lion ever got unruly with her or put its claws out, she'd grab it by the ear! She seemed to know instinctively that that would put the cub in its place," Colin says. "It reminded me of the way a grandmother might discipline a child." Except, of course, Beth controlled the bad cat with her mouth; human grandmas tend to pinch a whining kid with a thumb and forefinger. (Biting your grandkids is frowned upon.)

But for the most part, the relationship was soft-ish paws and gentle-ish mouths (*ish* enough for animals who specialize in hunting). "Beth loved them all," says her owner. "She had the time of her life being part of the pride." And she wasn't just a rough-and-tumble playmate, but, sometimes, a mom. "When there was an injured or orphaned single cub, it was incredible how her maternal instincts came to the fore. The same instinct showed up when we presented her with tiny serval kittens [spotted wildcats with big ears and stubby tails] or orphaned baby baboons." She'd go from cuddling and nuzzling one species to wrestling with another (though she ignored the MacRaes' domestic cats, for some reason).

Beth mothers two serval kittens.

"These were unique relationships that just sort of evolved." Her owners never set her up to be a cat lover. "It was in her all along."

Eventually, "Beth simply decided she was done with the lions," Colin says. She'd slowed down a bit in her maturity and perhaps didn't have the energy to deal with the near-wild animals anymore. She was also less enticed by the long, hot walks that the tourists and lions still enjoyed.

In her golden years, Beth has held on to her calm nature and friendliness toward other animals "despite her dangerous looks," Colin says. She still doesn't mind serval kittens and baby baboons playing all over her, and she lets them know when she's tired of their shenanigans with just a gentle push with her nose or paw. "She's a tremendous dog who wouldn't hurt a flea," Colin adds.

While Beth may be harmless, Colin points out that their lions are far from tame—no matter how much they interact with people when they're young. "You could raise a lion in a flat in London and it would still know how to hunt if you released it into the wild. We see their natural instincts rise up all the time—for example, during one walk they rushed off to chase a kudu, which barely escaped over a fence." The owners let such scenes play out naturally.

"Even if we wanted to, you can never really tame a lion," he says. Beth, of course, didn't have to. The cats were happy to have the extra playmate, regardless of her species and her lion-hunting ancestry. And Beth, for her part, didn't seem to know how to do anything but love them—teeth, claws, and all.

Romeo
and Juliet:
T HE C ANINE E DITION

H ERE ' S A BIT OF CANINE THEATER , A STORY THAT could have easily been penned by William Shakespeare— without all the "dosts" and "thous"—were the bard fan enough of dogs to cast them as dramatic leads.

Our four-legged stars are a skittish English pointer and a cheeky English setter mix—who stay together despite adversity and find their way to happily ever after. It's a powerful love story, so naturally the leads are named Romeo and Juliet. Fortunately, they give us a much happier ending than their fictional counterparts.

The beginning is a bit of a mystery, says Laura Santini, of the Holbrook Animal Rescue in Horsham, West Sussex, England. "We can only guess, but we presume they knew each other well already, that they were tied up somewhere together, and that they got loose or were set free."

Our lovers met not in the United Kingdom, but in Greece, on the island of Zakynthos. Imagine a sun-drenched day, two dogs trotting along the shore of the blue Ionian Sea, a broken lead attached to one of their collars. They race each other up a stony staircase and continue along a village street. No doubt they felt the pangs of hunger and thirst, but also the joys of freedom.

Somewhere along the way, the mood darkened. Someone, for reasons unknown, peered down the sight of a shotgun and began firing. Romeo, the setter, was hit by an explosion of pellets.

"It's tragic and inexplicable," Laura says. "This is a nice animal, not the type of dog that bites people or even chases chickens, so we can't imagine why someone would shoot him. Poor Romeo ended up with thirty-eight pellet wounds. It's amazing he survived."

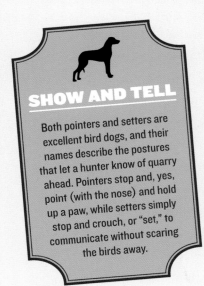

SHOW AND TELL

Both pointers and setters are excellent bird dogs, and their names describe the postures that let a hunter know of quarry ahead. Pointers stop and, yes, point (with the nose) and hold up a paw, while setters simply stop and crouch, or "set," to communicate without scaring the birds away.

Injured Romeo must have limped into a ditch to escape the shooter. Juliet remained nearby. Over the next few days, the ditch filled with water, but the dogs stayed put. Then, Juliet found her voice and began her soliloquy: barking and howling with intensity and persistence, clearly worried by the condition of her partner. Her angst rang through the streets.

"Little Juliet wasn't about to leave her friend, who was in that ditch for three days," Laura says. "We know because the local people could hear the barking, barking, barking, and kept phoning up a rescue center to report it." Finally, a rescue team came to investigate and found a hungry but wary Juliet and a weakened Romeo nearly dead, up to his neck in water.

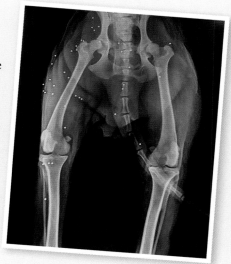

An X-ray reveals the pellets that wounded Romeo.

The rescuers pulled the wet dog from the ditch and loaded him into a car to take him to a veterinarian. Juliet, who initially cowered out of the people's reach, scampered in after him, unwilling to let her Romeo out of her sight.

Of course, the animals were separated for a time, by necessity. "Romeo was isolated from Juliet at the vet for a week, and he nearly died there," says Laura. "They could only get some of the pellets out of him. And the water hadn't done him any good. He pulled through, but Juliet was desperate without him."

When the rescuers saw how the two dogs acted when reunited, they knew they had to find them a home together. But they couldn't. For six months, the dogs languished at a Greek shelter. The story got around, eventually reaching the Holbrook Animal Rescue. Staff there decided they wanted to give the dogs a chance for a home in England. "We've moved animals great distances before," says Laura. "We find it hard to say no just because an animal is far away."

Soon, Romeo and Juliet were on their way, crated up and loaded onto a direct flight to London, where they were collected and driven to West Sussex. There, the Holbrook staff welcomed their new charges with excitement and love. Holbrook's rescue pups are treated well: They aren't kept in kennels but instead live in a house where they are not just allowed but *encouraged* to get up on the sofas and chairs. "We give them lots of treats, exercise, and affection," in addition to comfortable furniture, Laura says.

Romeo took easily to the other rescue animals at Holbrook, and by his playful exuberance, you'd never know he's still got a lot of pellets lodged in him. They seem to do him no harm and certainly don't slow him down. These days, "he runs and chases and wrestles; he doesn't sit around feeling bad for himself and nursing his old wounds," Laura says. "We hope he doesn't even know they're there."

Home at Holbrook.

Juliet, on the other hand, "is a quiet little girl, not very social." She'll often sit out the fun but always has an eye on Romeo. Laura says she thinks a lot about those days when the two dogs were waiting for help in Greece, "when she didn't leave him and was barking for help." It's quite something, she says, that such a silent scaredy-pup turned into a very vocal hero when it truly mattered.

Laura and the rescued pups.

The original plan was to adopt Romeo and Juliet out together. But it can be hard to place a pair of dogs, especially when one of them has trust issues. "They've had three tries, at three different homes, but poor little Juliet gets so frightened that she starts hiding or snapping if anyone tries to touch her," Laura says. "So the dogs keep coming back to us."

And that might be the best outcome anyway. "They're very happy here, even Juliet," says Laura. "We can do anything with her now, pick her up, cuddle her. She dances and spins around when happy. She's a silly thing. And she still adores Romeo—follows him around, lies on him like he's her pillow. Her love for him is extra special, perhaps because she almost lost him."

"We can't keep every dog that comes in, but these two have been through so much," Laura adds. "We wouldn't want them to suffer another move that didn't work out. If we don't find them the perfect place, then this will be their home for good."

And so, after a near murder, suspenseful days in hiding, a heroic rescue, and a long journey, Romeo and Juliet can at last celebrate their love triumphant. Now, if only dogs could take a bow . . .

The
Rottweiler
and the Wolf Pup

THE BIRTH OF THE WOLF PUP WAS TOTALLY UNEXPECTED. Staff at the Kisma Preserve in Mount Desert, Maine, thought the young adult pair too young to breed, so they weren't watching for a pregnancy. But then, out came a pup—born to a mother not yet mature enough to understand her role as parent. "There was no aggression," says the preserve's director, Heather Grierson, "but she had no maternal instinct whatsoever. She just didn't know what to do with it." Staff members at the preserve were used to bringing work home with them. In this case, Heather decided to offer her house to rear the baby animal, a helpless bundle with eyes still tightly shut.

Ulrok the rottweiler was there to greet them when Heather

arrived with her tiny charge. "Right from the beginning, he took excessive interest," Heather says. "I misinterpreted it at first, thinking he might get overly rough. Plus, he's huge and young and clumsy and might have hurt her by mistake. But he didn't. Instead, he was amazingly maternal." When the puppy whimpered, "he wanted to clean her top to butt, normally the mother's job. Ulrok simply took over. If he could have nursed her, he would have."

The wolf was completely responsive to the rottie's overtures, happy for the attention. And after realizing Ulrok wasn't content unless the pup was within licking reach, Heather let them share a bed so they could cuddle. The still-awkward pup tried to play with the big dog, and even licked Ulrok's mouth and chewed his tongue to try to get him to regurgitate food, as wolves do in the wild. "He'd neutralize her with his paw if she got too excited, but Ulrok was so patient with her!"

AGE-OLD HERDERS

The rottweiler, which originated in Germany, is one of the oldest herding breeds, dating back to the Roman Empire when the animals helped herd cattle for the Roman legion.

The pup's wolflike ways showed at mealtime as well. When it comes to food, wolves and well-fed domestic dogs are very different animals—not so much in what they like to eat, but in the lengths to which they'll go to protect their lunch. Any self-respecting wolf challenged for her food will curl her lip and snarl, eyes wild and stance wide. The pup did the same, and Ulrok respected her space. "Here was this five-pound pup growling at this one-hundred-twenty-pound dog, and he'd just back off and let her eat," says Heather. "People think that if you raise a wolf in captivity, it'll be like a pet dog. That's not true. They are hardwired in different ways."

That difference in temperament and behavior is one reason Heather wanted to make sure the wolf was exposed to her own species as soon as possible. So when the time was right, the pup was introduced to an old female wolf at the preserve named Morticia, who had been living alone for years. Happily, the two bonded from the start. "The pup breathed new life into the old wolf, who became more active having a young animal around. She was soon regurgitating food for her and teaching her wolf mannerisms and behaviors," says Heather. More convinced than ever that the pup knew what she was, the preserve staff felt confident in plans to integrate her into one of their captive wolf packs when the day came that elderly Morticia would no longer be there for her young companion.

As for Ulrok, whose breed is known for its herding and guarding instincts, he's now offered his parenting services to numerous animals at the facility, including tiger cubs, a baby gibbon, and even an injured leopard tortoise. "He really is the peace-love-and-happiness rottweiler of the world," says Heather. "He was just destined for this life."

The
Miniature Horse
and the Terrier

IF YOU SAW **D**ALLY THE **J**ACK **R**USSELL TERRIER AND Spanky the 32-inch miniature horse, you might suppose that the circus has come to town. And you wouldn't be that far off. These four-legged performers love the roar of the crowd. But their friendship is no act. For a dog and a horse, these two have a lot in common, including a special fondness for each other.

Francesca Carsen and her husband, Steve Rother, own the pair. Francesca, a horse veterinarian and behavior expert who lives near Spokane, Washington, swears that this real-life dog-and-pony show started with some daring theatrics: "One day, I was exercising Spanky with Dally watching intently, as she often did. I looked away for a moment. That's when Dally leaped up

on a step stool and, to my surprise, jumped up on Spanky's back!"

Before the duo met, Spanky was a troubled animal (not to mention shaggy and overweight). Francesca first saw him at a horse clinic that Steve, a trainer, was teaching in California. "He was a terror, a kicker and a biter. He had even drawn blood, taking a big chunk out of someone's arm," she recalls. "We aren't sure why—the woman who owned him was lovely. He was just a problem from the start, and she was at a loss."

On the verge of tears, the horse's owner had begged Francesca to take Spanky off her hands. The animal was dangerous and needed a lot of training and attention (and maybe a low-grain diet!). "At first, we said no because we had so many animals to care for," Francesca says, but before long she and Steve gave in and loaded the grumpy boy into a trailer that was already packed with three horses. Immediately, "Spanky flew right back out! He'd gone in biting, so the other horses kicked him out. We thought, *Oh my, even they can't handle him!*"

Fortunately, it turned out that Francesca could. "I worked with him a lot," she says, "and he got much better." She started exercising Spanky, "which helped him lose weight so that he felt good. I would often take him with me to the post office, a quarter mile away, and tie him outside. The locals thought he was a big dog! [Author's note: Sounds like they all needed glasses!] We both got our exercise jogging home."

She also used Steve's big-horse training methods on the little guy: establishing mutual respect, much-needed boundaries, and some affection (when he allowed it) for the animal that seemed nervous about trusting anyone or anything.

But Francesca says her training was only part of the solution. "When we got the puppy, things really changed for the better. Their relationship turned out to be a big part of his improvement. It was also great for the dog, giving her a reason to feel important."

As with Spanky, Francesca and Steve weren't immediately sold on taking custody of the runty Jack Russell terrier puppy that a friend offered. But warm-hearted Francesca eventually convinced her husband to add Dally to their family.

"She was so small when we got her that she could sit in the pocket of my sweatshirt," Francesca recalls. "Cute as a button, but there was all the barking." One likely reason for all the noise: The little dog's nerves were easily rattled.

Thankfully, once the fat, grouchy horse and the yappy pup found companionship in each other, things began looking up for both of them, and for their owners.

LITTLE HELPERS

Mini horses can be really, really tiny! Not all sources agree, but the smallest one may have been "Little Pumpkin," who stood 14 inches tall and weighed only 20 pounds. Larger ones, more the size of a big dog, have been trained as "guide horses" for the blind.

The friendship wasn't instantaneous. For a time, they'd be in the pasture together without showing much interest. Dally might nip playfully at the little horse's tail now and then, but Spanky wasn't convinced the dog was worth his time. It wasn't until Dally leaped up to meet Spanky on his level that the friendship took off. "It was all very surprising," Francesca says. "Most horses would not be okay having a clawed animal jump up on their back!"

Spanky remains a social pariah with the resident horses, just as he'd been on day one. But this special relationship has mellowed out both nervous Nellies, and given them things to do besides irritating other animals on the property. Now they each have a partner and a purpose. Inspired by Dally's leap, Francesca started training the animals to frolic in tandem, and they now put on shows across the country. They love working together to entertain and, unbeknownst to them, to help their owner educate the crowd about animal behavior.

Imagine, a horse with major trust issues who lets a dog proudly ride on his back like a little jockey. The two of them do jumps together, and Dally leaps back and forth over Spanky—when

Fame can be exhausting.

he's lying down—to everyone's delight.

Their theatrics even landed them a spot on *The Late Show with David Letterman* in 2015. Spanky was terrified by all the activity, Francesca says, but Dally, who loves the limelight, helped keep him calm and coaxed him over a jump on stage in front of millions of viewers.

A perfect performance.

Back home, sometimes all on her own, Dally will grab Spanky's lead in her mouth and tug until the horse follows her around. She's also been known to nose a big, blue ball over to the horse, but Spanky isn't all that interested in playing fetch. Even when it isn't showtime or playtime, Dally wants to be with "her" horse. "Dally comes with me in the mornings when I go out to feed the horses, and she goes to see Spanky first thing. Plus, she's always around when I'm exercising him," Francesca says.

They'll also flop down in a heap, the small dog's head on the miniature horse's belly, just being together. Sure, fans are great, but a lazy afternoon just hanging with your best buddy always beats the company of strangers.

The Pup *and* *the* Prisoner *Who* Set Each Other Free

HERE IS A TALE OF A MAN WHO SAVED A DOG. AND A dog who saved a man. Love is not a one-way street, you see.

Candido has a big family. His mother grew up in Puerto Rico with twenty-six brothers and sisters. The kids spent endless hours running around outdoors, and by Candido's generation, there were a lot of dogs running around with them. "I always had a tie with dogs," he recalls. "I've been able to connect with them in some ways better than with people."

Part of Candido's childhood was spent in New York City, and despite being poor, he had dogs there, too. His days revolved around them—feeding and walking them before school, rushing home afterward to play with them. He experienced the sorrow of having

Candido with Sam.

to give one away (because of apartment rules) and of watching one die of cancer. "It broke my heart to lose them," he says. He found himself depressed, and nothing but another dog seemed to make him feel better.

In some ways, dogs kept Candido out of trouble in his early years. But eventually, life in a violent neighborhood and a struggle with poverty pushed the young man to make some mistakes. "We were barely making it. My father worked several jobs to pay rent, my mother was a seamstress, always working. Still, we barely had enough food. Sometimes all I'd eat was cereal with water or toast sprinkled with sugar."

Unable to support her son, Candido's mother sent the boy to live with one of his aunts. He felt abandoned, hurt, and worthless. So when he saw a quick way to make money, he took it. He began selling drugs.

But he got caught. And he went to jail. For ten years.

Fast-forward a few years into his imprisonment. Candido was moved around a bit, but finally ended up at North Central Correctional Institution, a prison in Gardner, Massachusetts.

"That's where everything started to change for the good," he says. And the reason? Dogs.

Gardner had partnered with a nonprofit group called Don't

Throw Us Away in a three-year project that would benefit both canine and human participants. Prisoners without violent histories had the chance to care for and train the roughest dogs, from high-kill shelters, to make them adoptable. It makes sense: With thousands of inmates at minimum security facilities with time on their hands and space in their cells (and hearts), and millions of shelter animals needing foster homes and attention, why not bring these two populations together?

Candido immediately signed up. And after interacting with numerous dogs, he found his match: a black Lab mix named Sam.

"He was the worst of the bunch. He'd had the hardest time, the worst history," Candido recalls. "He'd been beaten a lot and was antisocial and scared. He was shaking in the back of his crate and didn't want anyone to get close to him. But somehow I knew I was the one to earn his trust."

Once the two were officially paired up, Sam's crate went next to Candido's bed in his cell. Candido was responsible for taking care of all of Sam's needs, and for training him (with help from a professional). At first, each time the inmate got close, the dog would growl. "I'd try talking to him, he'd growl. I'd try again, more growls. If I walked near him, he growled."

But Candido wasn't put off,

even when Sam nipped and snapped at him. "If you complain about the dog being too aggressive, they'll take it away. But I'm no snitch, and I wanted to save him because I understood him. He was in prison as much as I was. Mentally, emotionally, and physically, we were both locked up. I just had to find a way in."

It took time, patience, and a bit of blood, but Candido got to where he could crawl halfway into the crate without getting bitten. He kept going. "When I was finally able to hug and pet him, when he finally licked my hand, it made me cry," he admits. "I knew I'd broken through to him."

Within weeks, Sam was a new dog. He was still a bit defensive around other dogs, but he had opened up to people, which was a huge step. And soon, he started to show his happier, more boisterous side, even among other canines. Candido's commitment had turned a nervous, mistrustful animal into one that could become a wonderful pet.

MUTUAL BENEFITS

The U.S. correctional system had more than 2 million men, women, and young adults confined as of 2015. Our U.S. animal shelters take in nearly 4 million dogs every year. Programs that teach prisoners to train dogs (so the dogs can be adopted) are helping ease the burden on both sides.

Of course, the goal of Don't Throw Us Away is to get shelter dogs into "forever homes." The prisoners can't keep the animals, much as they may come to love them. So eventually, Sam had to move on. "It was bittersweet," Candido says, but he was thrilled to see the pup he'd nurtured find a happy home. "The whole experience was a blessing. It helped me in so many ways." And though over time, Candido trained six other dogs, he says Sam was the one that opened his eyes and stayed in his heart.

Candido with another canine friend.

Some inmates didn't want to work with a dog that had a bad history, that was troubled, that had been abandoned, he says, but "when I looked at Sam I saw myself, an animal who had had a bad time, who had been left behind and needed some understanding. I watched him change for the better. That made me want to get better." Seeing Sam move forward in such a positive way, "I said, the negative part of my life is over, too."

Since getting out of prison, Candido has been working, getting his GED (he hopes to someday work with animals), and helping to tend to his mother, who has cancer. "Sam was forgiving, and that was a great lesson for me," Candido says. "It's helped me to forgive my mother for sending me away as a kid. She had her reasons. I only have one set of parents and there's no sense in being angry about the past."

Meanwhile, he has a special five-year plan he came up with while living with Sam in his small cell. "I want to have a farm, a nice big space, primarily so I can have a bunch of animals," he says. "I want all kinds. But you can bet I'll have a lot of dogs."

The Husky and the Wee Kittens

PREY DRIVE IS A POWERFUL THING. IT'S ESPECIALLY strong among the most "primitive" breeds, whose wild instincts are still wound tightly into their DNA. They may be perfect angels with their owners at home, but out in nature, tempted by rabbits and squirrels and cats, their inner wolf can come to life.

That's how Lilo the Siberian husky was, once upon a time. In fact, when the three sisters who own Lilo first got the dog, they struggled mightily to train her to be civil, especially to other animals. The girls had to work with Lilo on boundaries and on food aggression. At the dog park, if there was a dog that was barking or very small, they'd take Lilo home, fearful that she'd attack it.

It was especially important to soften Lilo because the sisters,

Thoa, Thi, and Tram Bui, who live with their mom in San Jose, California, rescue a lot of small creatures that need some special care. "We've been doing it since we were kids," says middle sister Thoa. "Our parents weren't thrilled, but they tolerated it because we weren't doing anything bad." Also, she says, growing up as disadvantaged minorities (the family is Vietnamese), "we could relate to animals in need that didn't have a voice."

That desire to help remains strong. For a time, the three college students were using a rented trap to round up feral female cats in their neighborhood, and taking them to be spayed, funding the whole operation themselves. "We saw that these cats were having kittens on the streets—it was a real problem—and decided to do something to help," Thoa says. The girls fostered some of the kittens at home and, of course, ended up keeping one or two.

That gave Lilo some chaperoned exposure to felines, which helped her see small creatures as members of the pack instead of prey. And when the girls brought home a kitten called Misty, they were thrilled to find that Lilo treated it gently, even letting the kitten suckle on her. (Lilo had never had pups and had no milk to give, but that didn't stop Misty from trying!)

So when Rosie came into their lives later on, the sisters saw another opportunity to use Lilo as a surrogate mom. And in this case, Lilo's loving attention probably saved the tiny kitten's life.

Rosie was just two or three weeks old when the sisters took her in. Despite being motherless so early in life, "she was fine at first. She was moving around and meowing," says Thi, who stayed up all night trying to feed her.

But it didn't go well, and the next day, "she took a turn for the worse. She wasn't lifting her head, wouldn't eat. It didn't look good," Thoa says. Thoa ended up caring for Rosie that day (the sisters stagger their class schedules so one of them is always home to tend the animals), and having run out of options, she handed her off to Lilo, hoping the dog would respond as she had with Misty.

"I let them cuddle extensively; I didn't know what else to do," she says. "And then I saw Rosie start trying to nurse on Lilo, which told me she had the right reflexes, she could suckle, which was important." An hour after putting the animals together, Thoa says the kitten perked up and took a bottle. "It was such a fast turnaround! I was so relieved and happy. After feeding her through that day and night, I knew she was out of the woods."

The husky even began stimulating Rosie's digestive system by licking her, from belly to rump, to help her go to the bathroom. That's what a mother cat would do, and it's vital to the kitten's survival to get those, er, juices flowing.

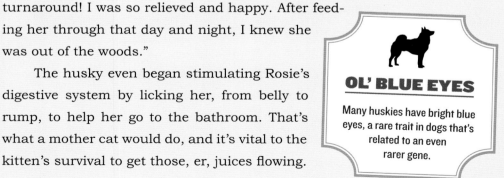

OL' BLUE EYES

Many huskies have bright blue eyes, a rare trait in dogs that's related to an even rarer gene.

"There's no doubt that it's because of Lilo that Rosie recovered and lived," Thoa says.

The sisters continued to be vigilant, making absolutely sure Rosie was in no danger from the once predatory husky as the kitten climbed all over her, kneading and licking. But it was clear that the formerly fierce Lilo loved Rosie as if she were her own pup, and she let the kitten do as she pleased.

Nowadays, Lilo and Rosie are regular playmates—chasing each other around and wrestling as roughly as Rosie will allow. "When they're not together, they look for each other," Thoa says. "And if Lilo isn't around, Rosie gets scared."

"This quality in Lilo of loving and comforting Rosie changed the way we saw her, and the way we saw people," Thoa adds. "It reminded us that there are different layers to everyone. And just because someone acts one way, that shouldn't define them forever. Lilo was aggressive toward other

Lilo (in red) and Rosie with husky friends Miko and Infinity.

A mixed-species hike.

animals before, but she became the best, most caring mom."

Because of her life with Lilo, Rosie is no ordinary cat. She's more like a dog, really, hanging out with several huskies without fear (the sisters have a second one, and a friend has another—though none of them is motherly like Lilo). They all go on walks and other adventures, including car rides and even kayaking. (A cat in a kayak: That's something you don't see every day!)

And at night, Lilo and Rosie curl up together, sometimes joined by Misty—who also remained part of the family after Lilo took her in—sleeping deeply after another day of cat-dog adventures. It's the perfect ending to the perfect story: beautiful Lilo, transformed from fierce predator to doting parent, dozing happily with both her babies by her side.

Yes, it's best to keep huskies away from cats as a general rule, says Thoa. "But can you push boundaries? Yes. We did and it worked out great. Lilo showed us anything is possible."

Clockwise from top left: Rosie cuddles up to Infinity; Infinity (left) and Lilo at the beach; Lilo and Rosie relaxing together; the dynamic duo on another adventure; and Lilo with Infinity (center) and Miko.

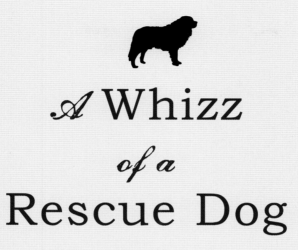

A Whizz
of a
Rescue Dog

SOME DOGS, IF THEY HEAR A FELLOW CANINE BARKING its head off, will bark back or just ignore the fool thing. Not this dog. Whizz listens. He decides if something is amiss. If so, he rushes to the rescue. A person crying out for help? Same response. Whizz just knows when there's trouble, and he loves to be the hero.

Whizz is a bicolored Newfoundland, weighing 180 pounds and standing 6 feet tall up on his hind legs. His specialty is saving lives in the water, and he never misses a chance to show off his superdog skills. You don't have to actually *be* in trouble to see Whizz in action, fortunately. If you're ever attending the annual Bristol Harbourside Festival in England, you'll want to be in a good spot when it's time for Whizz to do his thing. There, the dog exhibits his skills to cheering crowds, leaping from boats to pull swimmers—who are pretending to struggle, for the show—to safety. He's brought in hundreds of them, some to a boat, some to shore. And he's strong enough to do it twelve at a time (linked together in a human chain), if the need arises.

Most heroes don't start out life as superstars. Whizz certainly didn't. When David Pugh of Clevedon, North Somerset, first got the dog, the pup was just a year old and high-strung (his name describes his energy level), with potential behavior issues from a lack of attention and socialization in puppyhood. He'd also never set paw in a body of water bigger than a bathtub.

But in his second year, the dog became a whole new (water-loving) animal. It was affection and good training that changed him, says David, who has been working with "Newfies" for decades. "And for all my efforts, he's

Practicing a water rescue in the Bristol Channel.

TENDER TEMPERS

Newfoundlands are so gentle and loving with children that many wealthy folks in Victorian times bought one as a sort of "nanny dog" to keep an eye on the kids. Another Newfie tidbit: In the original *Peter Pan* novel, the dog, Nana, was based on the author's own Newfoundland, called Luath.

David and a very wet Whizz.

paid me back a thousand times over. He gave me everything he had, and he became the best I've ever worked with."

Whizz became the best in the world, in fact. Says David: "He took to it right away, learning in just months what it can take years for some dogs to pick up. And what's unique is that he will work, and work well, with other people, not just me. Only a true rescue dog will do that."

Pugh, Whizz, and the big dog's longtime handler, Victoria Welch, are part of the Royal Navy Reservists' Swansea rescue team and they train in the Bristol Channel. "He's always on duty, always alert," says Victoria, who has been Whizz's handler since 2008. "Whenever we're seaside, he has his eyes on the water to make sure all is okay."

Though the dog is a terrific performer, his abilities aren't just for show. Whizz has saved many lives, including those of two drowning dogs. Both pup rescues happened when David was walking Whizz—off duty. The first time, Whizz heard whining from a water tank and immediately ran toward the sound, found the dog struggling, and dragged him out. There were no instructions from a trainer. It was just Whizz doing what Whizz does.

Out on another walk, near a reservoir on a cold winter night, says David, "Whizz heard something and took off on his own again. It turned out to be an Irish Setter that had disappeared. He just jumped into the reservoir

Handler and hero take the leap.

and grabbed the dog by its scruff and swam to the edge." David pulled them both to safety. "The reservoir walls were steep," he says. "Whizz couldn't have done anything more on his own. But he saved that dog from drowning, there's no doubt. The owners were so thankful."

Saving fellow canines brought Whizz a bit of extra fame, but of course it's his human rescues that get the most attention—and he's had *nine* of them. Most have been swimmers who got tired or caught in a current, though occasionally the dog has taken a dip when someone fell off a dock (including, once, a person in a wheelchair). Whizz recognizes trouble—it's as much instinct as training—and knows what to do, his owner says.

The first at-sea rescue was of a young man who got cramps while swimming in the ocean, David says. "We got the call, went out in the boat, and found the lad. I went in with Whizz—the dog can't talk to the person to calm him or her, plus swimmers may panic and inadvertently drown a rescuer, so we never send the dog

alone. I do the talking, telling the person what's going to happen, then Whizz takes over." In perfect form, the dog, wearing a harness the swimmer could grab, circled the man, then pulled him to safety. "People are often embarrassed that they need rescuing," David says. "But they are so grateful to Whizz."

Victoria is grateful, too, for having the chance to spend time with such a special animal. Their connection was forged when she acted the part of a drowning swimmer and Whizz swam to her aid. "It was absolutely amazing to see him coming for me, to grab on to his harness, and have him pull me back to the boat. It was after that experience that I knew I wanted to work with this dog. That's where it all began."

Yes, the dog is schooled in lifesaving techniques. But it goes beyond training, Victoria says. "Right from the beginning, working with Whizz, he made me feel secure. He has that kind of presence. We trust each other one hundred percent."

Plus, "he's adorable. And he loves everybody," she says. That comes in handy when Whizz visits children's hospitals, which he does regularly through Newfound Friends, a charity that David set up in 1990. "He makes them so happy, even the worst-off ones," says Victoria. "It's amazing to watch him interact with sick kids so beautifully."

Whizz's expertise at making even chronically ill kids smile and his top-dog skills in speedily saving lives have earned him respect, fame, and awards—including the Dogs Trust Honour, the top canine prize in the United Kingdom. In early 2016, he received the Order of Merit for outstanding devotion from the PDSA (the country's leading vet charity). "There will never be another dog like him," says David. "But he is now training the next generation—including a closely related pup named Tizz—and the young ones definitely watch and learn from the master."

Whizz leads the way to safety.

Part of the Bents' vast menagerie, including pups Poppy (center) and Peggy (bottom), and Hollywood star Oreo the raccoon.

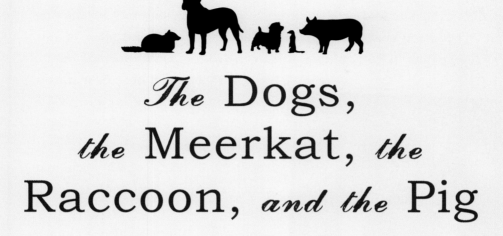

The Dogs, the Meerkat, the Raccoon, and the Pig

THE HOUSEHOLD OF SALLIE AND JOHN BENT OF Derbyshire, England, might just be the unlikely friendships capital of the world. The place is alive with a crazy mix of creatures who get along splendidly—including dogs, of course. Dull moments? Never.

The Bents' exotic collection includes funny little meerkats, kinkajous (rain forest dwellers that look like a lemur and a Chihuahua made babies), miniature pigs (that aren't so miniature), a gorgeous silver fox, an affectionate young binturong (a scruffy mammal that some people call a bearcat), skunks, armadillos, a Shetland pony, assorted creepy-crawlies, and Oreo, the pride of the pack, who's got Hollywood credits on his raccoon résumé.

The Bents run a company called Oreo and Friends, and they take their menagerie on the road. "We do all sorts of things, from giving special-needs kids encounters with animals, to visiting wounded soldiers, to providing animals for TV and films," Sallie explains. (I keep hoping to hear their little paws knocking on *my* door!) Sallie was a hospice manager for twenty years, caring for people at the end of their lives. Now she cares for animals and people, both, offering humans of all ages and circumstances a chance to learn firsthand about creatures they might not otherwise have a chance to meet.

Oreo

Poppy and Peggy, the Bents' two dogs, also turn out to benefit from such encounters, and they give back to their exotic-animal housemates with whole hearts. That's led to some special cross-species friendships.

Poppy is a Maltese-Chihuahua mix who has made quite a list of loving relationships to date, including bonds with foxes, skunks, raccoons, meerkats, "and many more," says her owner. The pup seems to be a mother at heart, and her maternal tendency first inclined her toward the famous Oreo, the raccoon who launched the Bents' business. Oreo served as the live-action reference raccoon for the Marvel superhero Rocket (voiced by Hollywood heartthrob Bradley Cooper) in the 2014 movie *Guardians of the Galaxy*. Oreo even got to attend the film's European premiere, riding on director James Gunn's shoulder.

In classic rags-to-riches style, Oreo didn't have the easiest start to life, and Poppy helped the Bents rescue the little guy, who'd been abandoned. "She always looked after Oreo when he was young," Sallie says. "Baby raccoons need constant heat, so Poppy used to let him snuggle right up to her. She was also the authority and, as Oreo got older, she would nip him to keep him in his place, just as a mother raccoon would do." Eventually, Oreo became too big and strong to romp safely with the loving little dog, and so he was introduced to another young raccoon as a playmate, Sallie says. But the family will always consider Poppy Oreo's first best friend.

Poppy and Timone the meerkat.

The next baby that Poppy "adopted" was Timone the meerkat, who also came to the Bents as a wee thing. Timone had lived with

a family in Wales as a solitary pet, but meerkats need a social group in order to thrive. The owners sent Timone to Derbyshire, and the Bents assumed he'd simply join the furry gang of meerkats already in residence.

Wrong! "He hated them, and they hated him!" Sallie says. "They were always fighting, and he was very alone." In the wild, a meerkat "mob" is usually made up of related individuals. Perhaps that's why Timone wasn't welcomed.

Then Poppy stepped in, seeming to understand Timone's need for a gentle companion. "Dogs are wonderful that way, taking in those that are rejected," Sallie says. "She took Timone on, and that was that. They did everything together from then on, sleeping, eating, even bathing."

"They were also quite protective of each other. They always presented a united front," Sallie says. Meerkats can be fierce, but with Poppy, "Timone was content. He'd rather be with the dog than anyone else."

Bath day.

Then there's Peggy. This little Staffordshire bull terrier was the runt of her litter, born partly blind and deaf, with three legs (one too few), eleven nipples (one too many), and a hernia. "Poor thing—she was completely, well . . . wrong," says Sallie. But none of that mattered once she was a member of the Oreo and Friends family. Among these animals, it seems differences are celebrated, not shunned.

Peggy and Primrose.

Peggy's most notable friendship must be the bond she's formed with a pig. Some call the animal a "micro" pig (born a runt, too) but this porker is anything but tiny now. No matter: Peggy accepts her pal Primrose as is.

"They've grown up together and gotten into all sorts of mischief," Sallie says. Recently, while

A not-so-micro friendship.

Primrose is such a pig.
(But Peggy will clean up.)

horsing (pigging? dogging?) around inside the house, one or both of them ripped a very expensive sofa. Whodunit? "The pig took the blame—my daughter jokes that Primrose might have to become sausages—but I think the dog did it, then framed the pig," says Sallie. Not surprising, both are currently "in the doghouse."

If the pup *does* lead their shenanigans, she is clearly forgiven. "The pig absolutely adores Peggy. With Peggy's poor eyesight and hearing, Primrose is her eyes and ears, and really takes care of her," Sallie says.

And together, dog and pig sometimes care for others. The two befriended an abandoned badger cub, protecting and sheltering it until the Bents were able to release it back into the wild.

Each evening, Peggy and Primrose put on a little romantic comedy. They may tussle briefly over their shared fleece blanket: Peggy sometimes drags it away, though Primrose always catches up and climbs on. But most nights, Peggy happily climbs up to the "top bunk," which in this case is her pig-friend's back, and flops belly down for the night.

"Yes, the terrier sleeps on top of the pig!" Sallie says. When Primrose was tiny, it was the other way around—piglet atop pup—but now they've switched places. "They keep each other warm, one way or another," says Sallie. Even on balmy summer nights, "they just have to be together."

Mix-and-match pals: Peggy also loves Timone.

Wicket with Zambian wildlife authorities.

The Dogs Who Sniff to Save Species

WICKET IS A BUNDLE OF ENERGY WRAPPED IN A SOFT, black coat. Her ears and nose twitch, her runner's muscles ripple, but her eyes stay focused on her handler. When she hears the command, Wicket knows what to do. Nose to the ground, the Labrador retriever begins her search, moving efficiently through the leaves, up and back, sniffing. There are plenty of potential distractions, but Wicket ignores them.

Suddenly, she sits, the signal that she's found the target. Aimee Hurt approaches and looks around, but sees nothing. "Where is it, girl?" Aimee asks. Wicket's nose dips back to the ground, and this time when her head comes up, there's something sticking to the end of her snout. "It's a rosy wolf snail, about two

A sniffer dog awaits his orders.

millimeters long," Aimee says. (That's smaller than a flea.) It's the species they're looking for, an exotic snail that has driven three quarters of Hawaii's native snails extinct since the 1930s. Such a tiny specimen "was an amazing find." Tracking snails may not seem like much of a job. But if you are a conservationist trying to preserve native species and habitats, finding the enemy—whether a snail or something more obviously menacing—is paramount.

But Wicket's sniffing talent goes well beyond snails. She knows twenty animal and plant scents that have allowed her to help efforts worldwide. She can find grizzly and black bear, wolf, and mountain lion poop. She knows the smell of California's endangered desert tortoise and sniffs out (but doesn't chase!) Franklin's ground squirrels. She's tracked the scent of Asiatic black bear scat in China, and Cross River gorilla dung in Cameroon.

Wicket is part of a group called Working Dogs for Conservation (WDC), based in Three Forks, Montana, of which Aimee is a founder. The group's sniffer dogs typically work on two kinds of projects. One kind aims to count the number of animals in a population or find out how they use the landscape—information that helps in resolving conflicts between developers and conservationists. The other project type focuses on exotic species—stuff that lives where it doesn't belong—helping scientists find and get rid of them.

Simply put, dogs home in on poop (and other smells) better and faster and more often than people do. Their noses are tens of thousands of times more sensitive than ours, with scores more olfactory receptors. A dog can separate out one scent from a mix of them, and can zoom in on, say, a bit of scat 30 feet off the trail. A ranger will likely only notice it—by eye—if it's less than 4 feet away. And even among dogs, Wicket is extraordinarily good at her job. "She knows more of these animal scents than any other dog in the program," Aimee says. "And she's always ready to work. She has that drive in abundance."

WDC uses the same processes to train their dogs that are used as drug- or mine-sniffing dogs, with a ball as the reward. "Except we have some special challenges," Aimee explains. "Our dogs work over very long periods, off leash, in natural wild environments. It takes a unique dog to ignore the distractions, and not to harass or injure the wildlife. Among a thousand dogs evaluated, only one will have what it takes to do the job."

SCAT FACTS

Tracking scat provides lots of information without ever having to trap (and thus stress out) real animals. Scientists get piles of data from scat samples, including DNA, hormones, and signs of parasites and disease.

Wicket, who was a "crazy" rescue dog when Aimee met her, turned out to be easy to train, enthusiastic, and smart. She's become Aimee's "right-hand man." At least half of the items Wicket has been trained to find are firsts—no dogs have ever tracked them before.

So, what is this dog actually accomplishing with her superior sniffing? Her nose inspired the relocation of a planned development away from a grizzly bear habitat in Montana's Centennial Mountains. In South Africa, she found the exceptionally rare geometric tortoise and located a long-lost female whose transmitter had fallen off. And the dog's efforts not only led to finding kit foxes where they hadn't been seen in forty years, but also pointed out the best kit fox habitat, which the Bureau of Land Management then bought for the animals' protection.

Now Wicket is the leading dog in a brand-new effort. WDC took its dogs to Zambia in Africa to practice tracking down snares—the wild animal traps that poachers use to catch often-threatened species. Aimee says WDC got real snares from Zambia to use in training. Once in the field, the dogs would learn additional scents associated with the traps—human scents.

But once her nose was on the ground, Wicket went even further. Aimee explains that where snares are hooked into trees, the tree gets wounded, giving off a certain smell. The same is true when twigs and branches are broken after someone tramples them. Without any specific training, "Wicket started clueing in on snapped branches, wounded plants, but not the types broken by

Another conservation hero.

elephants. She found combined scents of the metals plus human hands that helped lead us to the snares themselves. It was real detective work!" (It was also a great deterrent for poachers, who heard rumors that the dogs could identify the individuals who set the traps.)

As a final bonus, Wicket befriended the children in the village. "Dogs on the streets there are often kicked and teased, and kids aren't taught to care for them," Aimee says. "So when I invite kids to come pet Wicket or play fetch with her, they see there's another way to interact with animals." Having children learn how to be kind to other creatures? That might just be the best outcome of all.

The
Doberman
and the Gelding

A **GOOD FRIEND ALWAYS HAS YOUR BACK. A** *REALLY* **GOOD** friend also scratches it. Down in Peru, a horse named Contino does both for his favorite Doberman.

Leslie Stark got Contino from a horse dealer in Germany in 2011. The white Westfalen gelding was thirteen years old, and beautiful. After riding him for just a short time, "I decided he was amazing and I wanted him to go home with me!" she says. "He is calm, even a bit lazy. But he has a sparkle in his soul and a really special personality."

Leslie, a twenty-two-year-old college student who lives in Lima, found Contino a place to live at a local equestrian club and went each day to ride him. On one special visit, she brought a good buddy named Boss with her to meet the equine addition to the family.

Boss is Leslie's handsome male Doberman, who had always been confident around horses. Still, Leslie wasn't sure how the two would respond to each other as she and Boss walked into the stable. "I approached Contino to give him his usual greeting and carrot snacks, and Boss was right there with me. They smelled each other and seemed to connect right then. They were relaxed around each other from the start. I just knew it was the beginning of something special."

"A little to the left, please?"

Leslie began bringing Boss with her to see Contino every day. Quickly, the two animals developed an unusual relationship. They went from sniffing and standing around together to a more, er, intimate interaction: full-body massage.

It's hard not to giggle when the big horse lays those flabby lips on his Doberman friend and kneads the dog's back as if kissing him, or gives him a lick with that meaty slab of a horse tongue. He'll also pull his lips back and use his front teeth to nibble the skin, getting at an unseen itch

that, it appears, Boss desperately wants scratched. "Boss loves this attention," says Leslie, though if there are carrots being offered, Contino nibbles them first.

On days when he's preempted by vegetables, "Boss lies down beside him and waits patiently, sometimes chewing on a carrot himself. When his time comes, he wags his tail and turns his back end toward the horse's mouth," Leslie says, ready for his treatment.

While Contino is massaging Boss (and it's pretty much a one-way service, which seems to be okay with both animals), there's no point in trying to rush them, their owner says. If Leslie is in a hurry and tries to pull Boss away from his friend, she gets nowhere: "Boss stands strong and makes himself heavy so I can't move him at all."

Every relationship has its moments, of course. Occasionally, Contino gets a little too mouthy, biting a bit too hard. But over time, Boss has come to anticipate Contino's extra enthusiasm. "It seems Boss now knows when that's coming," says Leslie. "He'll give Contino a look" that stops problems before they start.

The two animals seem to enjoy each other's company, and will run circles in the ring with Boss holding the horse's lead. Sometimes they romp around together in free-form play (although

Sharing a point of view.

Leslie limits these more enthusiastic games, since the pup could get trampled by mistake).

Their main interaction remains the horse-to-dog rubdown. It may not seem like much, but "it's very special because it shows a lot of trust and caring between them," Leslie says. "Each has really gotten to know the moods and attitudes of the other." Contino knows what to do for Boss and Boss really appreciates the love, always coming back for more.

Perhaps it's not the most balanced relationship: Contino is almost always the giver. But if it brings happiness to both horse and dog—which Leslie says it does—and keeps Boss relaxed and itch-free, then good for them. Who are we to judge the inner workings of a friendship so unlikely?

The Devoted Dachshund and Her Feline Charge

RUTH AND IDGIE HAD A ROUGH MORNING. THE TWO were discovered, probably not long after they'd been abandoned, nestled together atop a seething black mass. Ants. The dachshund could have escaped the ghastly swarm but she'd chosen not to, because her cat friend didn't have that same choice. Partially paralyzed, Ruth was stuck. And so Idgie stuck with her.

But when Animal Control eventually collected the pair, they followed protocol and separated cat from dog. Big mistake. Despite any weariness from the stressful experience, both animals had strong enough lungs to let their rescuers know how they felt about being apart. And very quickly, protocol or no, they were reunited. And the crying stopped.

That's where Jackie Borum comes in. She's the manager at Hollywood Houndz Boutique and Spa in Lake Mary, Florida, which handles animal adoptions in addition to selling products and pet services, and she agreed to take in the animals—permanently. She named the pals Ruth (cat) and Idgie (dog), for the best-friend characters in the film *Fried Green Tomatoes*, and created a fenced-in space for them in the shop.

Something was clearly amiss with the cat. Ruth struggled to walk—her legs couldn't support her. She had to drag herself with great effort to get around, her front paws bent at ninety-degree angles. So Jackie had her veterinarian take a look. He said there were a couple of things going on. Ruth was diagnosed with neurological myopathy—a progressive degenerative disease of the spinal cord—as well as an autoimmune disorder that affects her red blood cell count. "She was, and still is, very fragile," Jackie says.

PET STATS

According to the Humane Society of the United States, more households have dogs (54 million) than cats (42 million) as pets, but people who have cats tend to have more than one. By the numbers, that makes cats, at 86 million total animals (versus 78 million dogs), the most popular pet in the country!

But Idgie seemed to sense Ruth's needs from day one, giving her plenty of attention, bringing her toys, nuzzling and playing with her, and of course hunkering down with her at both naptime and nighttime. "They are so tight! It's quite a thing to see how they are together," Jackie says.

Considering where things started, the animals are very pampered in their new life. Especially Ruth, who gets all-day care from the boutique staff (she requires medicine, has her blood sugar monitored, and even gets acupuncture) as well as gourmet food (which Idgie happily tests for quality). To

complete the royal treatment, Idgie will even pull Ruth around in a little cart like a princess. And both get lots of love from clients and visitors. They've become quite a draw, in fact. "It's crazy," says Jackie. "We've had people come in from all over the United States, Canada, from Peru and France, and elsewhere hoping to pet them and take a photo with them. Idgie especially eats up the attention."

Meanwhile, despite her limitations, Ruth is no meek kitty. "If life is about how feisty you are, this cat is going to be around for a long time," Jackie says. "She's very demanding; she tells you when she wants something." And playtime can get pretty rough— dog and cat wrestle around and Ruth will slap-slap-slap the pup's muzzle if her friend annoys her. It's a relatively soft punishment, but it gets the job done.

Jackie says "don't be fooled" into thinking Ruth is weak. "If she thinks she's getting a bath, she'll use not just her mouth but all four of those legs to protest." (Picture this: Ruth and Idgie get joint baths. In the same basin. Jackie declined to share a photo of

that mad-cat scene!) But even though it seems like the tough kitty can take care of herself, Idgie stays by Ruth's side and protects her. "If another dog comes into the shop, Idgie is right there letting them know 'Be warned, this is my cat!'"

The pair still strongly objects to being separated, even briefly. "Sometimes we'll take Idgie out for a walk or for ice cream [she's not too picky about flavor], and she'll keep wanting to pop her head in the shop and look at Ruth between outings," Jackie says. "It's like she needs to see the cat's okay and tell her, 'I'll be right back!'"

With all of her health problems, no one can say how Ruth will fare over time, but as long as her quality of life is good, Jackie says, they'll keep her with her best friend. The two have become international celebrities on the internet and are the faces of Project Paws of central Florida, Jackie's nonprofit organization that raises medical care funds for rescue animals.

"Their story has drawn a lot

of attention to the issue of unwanted and abandoned animals," she says. "Because of Ruth and Idgie, we have been able to help thousands of others like them, animals in need. These two are wonderful ambassadors."

And, if I may say, utterly irresistible, too.

Down for the night.

The
Goat *and*
the Pit Bull

JULIE AND NATE FREE LIVE NEAR TULSA, OKLAHOMA, on the dead end of a rural road, where horses and fishponds and barking dogs set the scene. And goats. Nate has a bunch of them. Late one April night, while away on a trip, he called his wife and asked her to please check on a certain goat that was soon to give birth. The goat was a first-time mama and he was worried about her.

"It was midnight," Julie recalls, "and yes, the goat was fully in labor."

"Mama delivers the first baby," Julie says, "and it isn't moving. The mom runs to the other side of the pen, not interested in him, so I scoop him up and chase after the mother because

suddenly she's having another one. And then, a third! In all my husband's years of owning goats, he's never had triplets before." When goats have three kids, as they're called, one usually doesn't make it. (Some mammals and birds have evolved to have an "extra" baby as insurance—to boost their chances of ending up with at least one healthy offspring.) Unfortunately, that seemed the likely fate for that first kid.

"I called my husband and said I didn't know if this little boy was going to make it. But of course, I had to do everything I could." Julie carried the runt, still motionless, into the house and laid him on a towel on the floor so she could go get a heating pad.

Julie and Nate have five dogs, but at the time all were in their crates for the night. Except Piper. "Piper is the only well-behaved one," Julie says, laughing. She's laughing because Piper is a pit bull, and everyone expects if you have a bad dog and a pit bull, they must be one and the same. "She's just not what you'd expect," Julie says. "If the other dogs are in an argument, she'll go hide in the closet." Not exactly the ferocious monster of repute.

"So Piper is watching this whole scene. And then she starts acting very strangely," Julie says. "She's looking at the goat, then looking at me and making a very low *woof*, then looking back at the goat, back at me, the *woof*, over and over." Julie realized Piper wanted to inspect the animal, so she gave her the okay.

Piper went straight to the goat and began licking him. "She licked and licked it all over, and after a while, the goat started to come around! It's as if it suddenly came to life."

Piper and GP ("Goat Puppy") were like mother and son after the dog revived the little goat that night.

Piper would clean GP's milk-coated chin and lovingly wrap herself around him as he napped. GP would take dog walks with Piper, Julie, and Nate—a goat on a leash. "Neighbors would just stop and stare," Julie says. And when Piper was in agility training—running and climbing and leaping over obstacles—GP was right there with her, trying to follow her lead.

At one point, unfortunately, GP began dragging one of his legs. He may have gotten caught up in the fence or perhaps one of the bigger goats injured him—Julie and Nate aren't sure. At first they hoped it would heal on its own, but instead the circulation became so bad that it was clear it needed to be amputated.

"Now, I'm used to working with small-town vets," Julie says. "And they put up with a lot from me. But when I show up on a Sunday with a broken goat and a pit bull, saying, 'This is Piper's goat and she keeps him calm and needs to stay with him'—they might have thought I'd finally gone crazy."

Still, the vet allowed Piper in the room during the operation on GP. And at one point, Piper put her paws up on the operating table, trying to see what was going on. "She was asking, 'What are you doing to my goat?'" says Julie.

As GP recovered from surgery and began running around again, Piper continued to watch over him, play with him, and favor him over the other animals. "We have a pit bull that loves a goat, and vice versa," Julie says. "It's like nothing I've ever seen before."

Piper's love of GP, and GP's love in return, has brought a special joy into Nate and Julie's lives. "GP has a home forever here with us," Julie says. And Piper certainly isn't going anywhere. After all, she's got her goat.

The
Loving
Labrador

THE OTHER DAY, I WAS ON THE PHONE WITH A LOVELY lady named Ladoreen ("Laddie") Reeb, and suddenly she started laughing like a young girl. Almost giggling. It turned out there was a big yellow dog licking her face. I'm not sure how she kept the phone to her ear with Dresden, a Labrador retriever, half in her lap. She gave the pup a bear hug (a witness told me) and called her a "rascal," before turning her attention back to my questions.

"What was that all about?" I asked her.

"That was about love," she replied.

Laddie, who is eighty-eight years old, has advanced lung disease. She is a hospice patient, meaning she is nearing the end of her life and is trying to live it out as comfortably and pleasantly as she can. These days, she gets nursing assistance with a lot of things, and her mind works better drumming up memories from fifty years ago than it does recalling yesterday's activities.

Laddie chats with Dres.

But one thing that seems to stick in Laddie's mind is Dresden. "She's such a lovely dog," Laddie tells me. "She's perfect. Her coat is so soft, so beautiful. And her tail is always going! She's my friend. She visits me sometimes here at the home [an assisted living facility in Seattle] and it's always a high point of my day."

Those visits can really help to ease feelings of abandonment and loneliness that a lot of people with severe memory loss have, says Shakur Sévigny, a spiritual counselor to Laddie and other patients. The dog also brings great joy, which Shakur sees as "a healing state of being."

Laddie certainly sounds joyful as she tells me what Dresden is up to. "She's sitting here right now, looking at me, resting against me. And there goes her tail again!"

Dresden is a therapy dog, trained through a nonprofit called CCI (Canine Companions for Independence), who gives most of

her time and love to hospice patients around Seattle. She's been working since November 2007 with terminally ill people of all ages. Does someone who is dying need a different kind of comfort than someone who will recover? Perhaps. Accepting death, and focusing on the life that's left, can be a difficult transition. Many people believe our animals "know" when we're stressed out or distraught, and that they even sense when we are nearing death. Dresden is extremely sensitive to human feelings that way, partly from training but partly from something innate. Not all animals respond to others' subtle emotions the way she can.

Just what Dresden actually understands is, of course, unknown. But what she *does* is exactly right. "She's a calming presence," says Maureen Horgan, a social worker and executive director of Gentiva Hospice, who has been Dresden's handler for nearly a decade. "She knows how to position herself so a bed-ridden person can reach her; they love to stroke her soft ears. If asked, she'll get up on beds even of the most fragile people. Or she'll just lie at a person's feet if that's what they need right then."

A few days after chatting with Laddie, I speak to another fan of Dresden's, Christy Bergen. Despite a sadness that will never go away, Christy is able to share happy stories about her beloved little girl, Kaylie. Kaylie passed away in 2012 at age eight of a brain tumor, but in the months before she died, as a hospice patient, she got to know Dresden the way Laddie is doing now.

"Dresden knew exactly how to respond to what a kid wants and needs," says Christy, who now volunteers for Peyton's Ranch, an organization that brings animals to kids with brain tumors. "When she started coming to see Kaylie at home, it was really special. She would do whatever my daughter wanted. She would sit in Kaylie's lap or let Kaylie dress her up, or she might just sit calmly with her when Kaylie needed quiet time. She was perfect."

According to her mom, Kaylie had never been that enamored of dogs. "She was all about cats. We had a 'kitty room,' where we'd foster sometimes six or seven from the local shelter at a time.

EVERYONE'S FAVORITE

According to the American Kennel Club, the Labrador retriever (which comes in yellow, brown, or black) has been the most popular breed in the United States since 1991.

She was always in there giving them love." But Dresden offered Kaylie the very best a dog could give. "They really connected. Between Dres and the cats, Kaylie's focus was really on animals up until she died."

The little girl was not without human friends, of course. But as Kaylie's disease progressed, she started to lose mobility, which made it hard for her to run and play the way her friends did. "That's when Dres became so important," says Christy.

Dresden certainly has a peppy side that

Kaylie, with Dresden.

brings joy to those who seek it. But it's her calmness, an ability to be around extreme noises, around people crying from pain, even around animals she might like to chase (like Kaylie's cats), that really makes her special. "It's hard to train a dog to handle all that," Dresden's handler, Maureen, says.

Dresden also brings comfort to the staff who take care of hospice patients. "Nurses are trained to keep people alive. Realizing all your patients are going to die is hard," Maureen says. "It can be a profound experience. And having Dres there as part of it—sometimes a nurse will just lie down with her to get through an emotional day—there are no words for how helpful that is."

People who meet Dresden often say she has sad, soulful eyes, her handler adds. "I see patients reflecting on what's happening to them as they look into her eyes. Sometimes her being there helps them to open up about their feelings." The dog can also be a bridge to conversation about loss after a loved one is gone, she says.

But Christy says, for Kaylie, at least, Dresden wasn't necessarily there to dig up her feelings or help her to express her fears, as therapy animals can sometimes do. "Dres was the highlight of our days, the fun in Kaylie's life. That's the way we saw her. She brought our little girl joy. Because of that special dog, Kaylie had a few more chances just to be a kid."

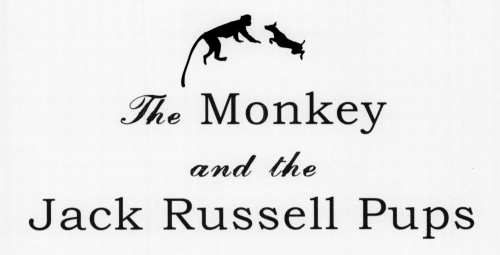

The Monkey
and the
Jack Russell Pups

SOMETIMES WE CONNECT WITH PEOPLE VERY BRIEFLY, but our short dealings end up being unexpectedly significant in our lives.

I remember a special friendship like that. I was probably nine years old, and my mother and I were shopping at a department store. I spotted another little girl with her mom looking at clothes on a nearby rack. We peered at each other between the dresses, shyly, as our mothers slid hangers. I was nervous, but I finally scrounged up the courage to go up to her and introduce myself. Soon enough, our moms were chatting as we sat on the floor and giggled below them. Within an hour my mom and I were driving to my new pal's home to have lunch and go swimming in their pool.

I don't know why, but that was the only day I spent with that girl. I can't even recall her name. But there have been times when I've conjured up that memory to help me break through shyness, when I have to introduce myself to someone I don't know. (Journalists have to do that a lot!) Knowing that my department store "bravery" led to a happy, if brief, friendship, has given me courage along the way.

That memory came to me when I heard about the temporary but intense friendship between a young monkey and a pair of puppies at a wildlife center in England. Though they spent limited time together, the playful experience gave the little orphaned primate confidence and some social skills that she'll use for the rest of her life.

Mubi is a drill monkey—a type of baboon. Her species is incredibly rare: There may be as few as 3,000 left in the wild in just a handful of African countries, and fewer than 50 in captivity outside of Africa. They are highly endangered. So at a place like Port Lympne Reserve, when a mother drill rejects her two-week-old baby, the staff steps in. In this case, the plan was to hand-rear Mubi and return the monkey to her parents once she was weaned.

Simon Jeffery has had a life most kids would envy: He grew up in wild animal parks, with zookeepers as parents. He himself has been a keeper of primates for the past twenty years. At Port Lympne, which is less than two hours from London but filled with wild creatures from far and wide, he shares his days with some 1,000

Other friends: A young antelope (bottom) and a safe-to-chew gorilla.

animals, including 160 primates representing 16 different species. The enclosures are large and natural, and when possible, animals are returned to the wild, so he feels good about the work he is doing.

Simon likes exotic animals, of course, but he enjoys regular old dogs, too, and a couple of years ago he brought home two Jack Russell terriers, Ian and Daisy. That was the same week he started toting Mubi home with him at night to give her the near-constant care a young monkey needs.

The timing couldn't have been better, because monkeys and Jack Russell puppies, it turns out, make great playmates. "Here you have two very social kinds of animals, young enough [and with small enough teeth] to have fun without hurting each other," Simon says. "The night they all met, I had Mubi in my lap and

was feeding her. The pups were six weeks old, and they smelled something interesting, so they kept jumping up on the couch to see what I had. And that's when Mubi grabbed someone's tail."

That tail-grab told Daisy and Ian that the little creature—not quite puppy but likeable just the same—wanted to play, "and then it was one big game. Mubi would tap a pup's nose and then run off. The dogs would chase. They'd try to grab Mubi's stumpy tail, so she'd turn and jump on them. She was such a perfect little monkey, leaping from my lap to the couch to the dogs and back out of their reach again. It was a good bit of rough-and-tumble, healthy for all of them."

"Normally, we'd want to introduce a little brother or sister to a monkey like Mubi," he says, "but we didn't have one at that time. So that social life with the dogs was quite nice for her." And it wasn't just nice: For young mammals, playtime is both physically and mentally useful—teaching skills for getting along in a group hierarchy later. It may look like they're just chasing, teasing, and stealing one another's toys, but such silly romping is actually educational.

Learning social skills is particularly vital for drills, which live in groups of up to 200 of their own kind. Mubi's schooling was uniquely interspecies, of course, but "these were similarly sized animals, so each just saw other babies to wrestle and chase," Simon says. Puppy-monkey kindergarten lasted about three hours a night for four months; Simon's living room was the playground.

Meanwhile, during the day, Simon would bring Mubi back to the reserve to interact with her parents through a screen. Putting the family back together later would depend on their developing a good relationship. Her father, Nebosia, seemed curious about the mini monkey on the other side, but, for a time, her mother, Yola, remained indifferent. (First-time primate moms are often flummoxed by the baby, especially if they struggle with nursing. The confusion can lead to rejection, as it did with Mubi. Happily, Yola soon had another baby in her arms, and the second time she took to motherhood like a pro.)

Mubi's time with the puppies has ended, and the monkey is thriving. She is again among the drills, getting along with her parents and monkeying around with her siblings. Meanwhile, Daisy and Ian have a lot more love to give, and don't seem to mind where it goes. Their attention turned next to a young antelope at the reserve that was being hand-reared like Mubi. "That went well, too," says Simon. "They really kept an eye on her, rushing over if she fell down to make sure she was okay. The antelope would run with them as she would with her own herd."

Getting over shyness, learning to be friends, running with the herd. I owe my thanks to that little girl at the mall for giving me my start. Mubi, and other animals at Port Lympne Reserve, can thank two rowdy Jack Russells for sharing their playful attitude and their openness to friendships of all sorts.

References

My work finding these animal stories includes scouring the web for tidbits that get me moving toward an original source. Sites that have provided source names or have given me an idea to pursue include:

Facebook (where some of my featured animals have their own pages)
Instagram
The Daily Mail
The Daily Mirror
The Daily Telegraph
Bored Panda
Buzzfeed
Ohmidog.com
ABC and NBC News (videos)

Some dog breed information came from the AKC (American Kennel Club); other basic animal information may have come from Defenders of Wildlife, Panthera, *National Geographic*, merriamwebster.com or britannica.com.

SCIENTIFIC PAPERS AND NEWS ARTICLES

asknature.org/strategy/2ecc0bc750f8f5a2424d1d6405ebb992

chathamdailynews.ca/2015/02/16/popeye-the-dog-gets-hero-award-for-saving-17-horses

journals.plos.org/plosone/article?id=10.1371/journal.pone.0143047 ("Dogs evaluate threatening facial expressions . . .")

livescience.com/27976-coyotes.html

livescience.com/27406-meerkats.html

mentalfloss.com/article/48681/how-can-owls-rotate-their-heads-270-degrees-without-dying

mentalfloss.com/article/68473/15mysteriousfactsaboutowls

nature.com/news/ancient-wolf-genome-pushes-back-dawn-of-the-dog-1.17607

nature.com/news/dog-s-dinner-was-key-to-domestication-1.12280

nature.com/nature/journal/v495/n7441/full/nature11837.html

news.nationalgeographic.com/2016/01/160105-chameleons-tongue-speed-animals-science

ngm.nationalgeographic.com/2015/05/dolphin-intelligence/foer-text nytimes.com/2012/02/05/magazine/wonder-dog.html?_r=0

pets.webmd.com/dogs/features/ear-cropping-and-tail-docking

phys.org/news/2015-12-tale-dogs.html

science.sciencemag.org/content/348/6232 (*Science*, issue 6232, various articles)

smithsonianmag.com/smart-news/humans-may-have-domesticated-dogs-24000
-years-earlier-thought-180955374/?no-ist

today.com/health/little-angel-rescue-dog-helps-doctors-monitor-girl-during
-surgery-2D11765780

washingtonpost.com/news/innovations/wp/2016/01/29
/dogs-may-have-evolved-to-handle-our-bad-tempers/

well.blogs.nytimes.com/2015/04/16/the-look-of-love-is-in-the-dogs-eyes

OTHER WEB SOURCES

aspca.org/animal-homelessness/shelter-intake-and-surrender/pet-statistics

bjs.gov/content/pub/press/p14pr.cfm

bmdca.org/breed_education/pdf/09_bernese_activities_draft.pdf

caninejournal.com/pit-bull-facts

desertmuseum.org/books/nhsd_mustelids.php

dogcare.dailypuppy.com/husky-dogs-blue-eyes-7010.html

dogtime.com/dog-breeds/mastiff

express.co.uk/news/weird/445650
/Puppy-love-Dangerous-dog-is-tamed-after-falling-in-love-with-a-goose

gentle-newfoundland-dogs.com/newfoundland-dog-facts.html

guidehorse.com

guidingeyes.org

ingoundelse.de/ingo-and-friends

patient.info/doctor/mastocytosis-and-mast-cell-disorders

petplanet.co.uk/dog_breed_profile.asp?dbid=60

prisonpolicy.org/reports/pie2015.html

weaselwords.com/ferret-articles/history-of-the-ferret

zooatlanta.org/drill_monkey

Acknowledgments

As the *Unlikely* series continues to grow, so, too, does my appreciation for those who help me find the stories, make them sing on paper, and get the final product out into the world. In the case of *Dogs*, I owe extra-special thanks to:

My researcher, Kate Horowitz, an awesome human being without whom these books would be about half as long and not nearly as varied and fun;

My "first eyes" editor, Lynne Warren, a super talent and friend who can always make what I've written read better while making me feel better about what I've written;

Three fabulously smart ladies: Elizabeth Ataly and Karen Font, for help with translations, and Melanie Carlos, for extra research assistance;

My writing tribe, *Literature or Chickens*, for helping me cope with both work and life and for complimenting my ankles when I'm feeling insecure;

And of course, the generous people who shared stories and photos of the special dogs in their lives, and the various animal-rescue organizations involved, for giving me fresh fodder for this *Unlikely* volume.

At Workman Publishing, I'm eternally grateful to my gentle editor, Sam O'Brien; my dogged photo editor, Michael DiMascio; my talented production editor, Beth Levy; and my patient publicist, Chloe Puton, for all of their many efforts on my behalf, plus thanks to Tae Won Yu and Ariana Abud, for lovely illustrations and design work. I'm lucky to have such a passionate and devoted team to help make the *Unlikely* series a more likely hit!

Finally, thanks to my husband, John, for making me laugh every day; to our families here, there, and abroad for loving me and giving me my kid fixes as needed; to our friends and neighbors, who make sure we occasionally socialize with other humans; and to the three crazy canines who remind me daily who the stars really are.

Jennifer S. Holland